Rotation Basics

A Practical Guide for Sunday School and VBS

CONCORDIA PUBLISHING HOUSE · SAINT LOUIS

3558 S. Jefferson Avenue, St. Louis, MO 63118-3968
1-800-325-3040 • www.cph.org

Edited by Mark S. Sengele

This publication may be available in braille, in large print, or on cassette tape for the visually impaired. Please allow 8 to 12 weeks for delivery. Write to Lutheran Blind Mission, 7550 Watson Rd., St. Louis, MO 63119-4409; call toll-free 1-888-215-2455; or visit the Web site: www.blindmission.org.

Manufactured in the United States of America

Your comments and suggestions concerning the material are appreciated. Please write to Concordia Publishing House, 3558 S. Jefferson Avenue, St. Louis, MO 63118-3968.

1 2 3 4 5 6 7 8 9 10 18 17 16 15 14 13 12 11 10 09

Table of Contents

Introduction

In recent years, we've been hearing a lot about rotation models. Recent converts to rotation glowingly tell you about the increases in attendance or the ease of volunteer recruitment. They may forget to tell you about the intense advanced planning involved or how long the transition took. Further confusing the discussion is what is meant by "rotation." Distinct and important differences separate the various rotation styles or models. How each model is used greatly impacts both the participants and the leaders.

Rotation Basics seeks to help eliminate some of the confusion surrounding rotation models by giving you a glimpse of a few different rotation models, each presented by someone with experience using that particular model. While most of the chapters apply the rotation model to Sunday School, rotation has been used effectively in the Vacation Bible School setting for many years.

As you consider the switch to rotation in your congregational children's ministry, we encourage you to read along and consider which model or models work best for your particular setting. Each author in *Rotation Basics* shares their personal experience with a specific rotation model or adaptation of a model and how it works in their congregation. Through their practical experience, we pray that you will find guidance in deciding how to best implement rotation in your situation. May God bless your work as you share the saving message of Jesus Christ with His little ones.

1

Why Rotation?

By Mark Sengele

A New Way of Thinking

A few years ago, when Concordia Publishing House made the switch to only offering a site-rotation Vacation Bible School kit, I had a phone call from a concerned customer who knew me from my work in a neighboring congregation. They couldn't believe that CPH would make this change and not consider how it would affect their longtime customers. They asked me to please help them understand how this new site rotation was going to work.

As I began to describe the elements of site rotation and how it worked in VBS, suddenly the customer stopped me and said, "Oh, *site rotation*, is that what you call what we've been doing for the past five years?" As it turned out, this congregation had already been using many elements of site rotation for some time, they just didn't recognize site rotation by name.

This same story is doubtlessly true for many congregations. During the week of Vacation Bible School, they divide kids into groups, moving them from station to station for things like snacks, games, music, and so forth. They've been conducting a rotation format, but never knew its formal name. And while this rotation format has worked successfully for them in Vacation Bible School, they've probably never considered making the rotation transition for Sunday morning.

Eyes Wide Open

While Sunday School may have a long history and tradition in many congregations, it has suffered from a steady decline in student and adult participation for a number of years. Even congregations with robust Sunday School attendance ten years ago have seen their numbers dwindle and their volunteers burn out. Sadly, for some, that has meant giving up on Sunday School altogether. Some continue to muddle through, afraid to change, but not willing to give up. Others have changed their way of thinking about Sunday School and have seen significant results.

Among the most frequently heard statements regarding the decline in Sunday School, a few stand out. The first is, "Sunday School is boring"; followed closely by, "It's impossible to find dedicated volunteer teachers." I might also add, "Parents aren't committed to bringing their children to Sunday School." Whatever the cause, many have turned to one of the rotation models as the solution.

As you consider adapting a rotation model, take time for a brief "reality check." If your most frequently heard statement concerns attendance/boredom, how will rotation become a solution? Studies have shown than any change results in renewed interest for a brief period of time. But if you are going to invest the time and energy into making fundamental changes to the way you conduct Sunday School, you want more than a short-term increase in attendance. Thankfully, most of those who have made the transition to rotation report a sustained increase in attendance and interest among children.

The other most often heard Sunday School issue is the lack of volunteers. While rotation models allow you to recruit volunteers for very specific tasks, and often for shorter time periods, the overall number of volunteers required can be significantly greater than with a traditional Sunday School format. For example, the number of Shepherds required to lead the small groups will likely be equal to the number of teachers in a traditional Sunday School. Then you still need to recruit your Rotation Teachers, Craft Leaders, Snack Coordinators, and so forth. In other words, while each volunteer may have less of a commitment, rotation requires a greater total number of volunteers to effectively conduct the program.

Unfortunately, no program or model can "fix" a lack of commitment on the part of parents. We can, however, continue to pray for those who need an extra measure of encouragement to get involved. Work together with your pastor and other church leaders to develop a culture of biblical scholarship within your congregation that encourages those of all ages to be involved in the study of the Word.

Moving Forward

As you realistically examine your Sunday School program, you may decide that all you really need are some minor tweaks to your existing setup. Perhaps you might borrow one element of a rotation model to use in your congregation.

Other programs may require a more drastic makeover. As you consider the depth of these changes, take the time to first evaluate what you are doing. Then, move forward by examining the rotation models that follow and adopting the model or models that best fit your situation.

2

Making the Rotation Transition

By Christine Eid

You've heard a lot about rotation Sunday School, and you think it might be the direction you want for your children's ministry needs. Now what? What are the steps you need to take as you transition to a new educational model? Who needs to be involved?

To make the transition as smooth as possible, consider these steps.

Create a Team to Work Together

Sunday School has a long history. For most congregations it is their first, and perhaps only, children's education program. Likewise, Vacation Bible School is often among the busiest weeks at any congregation. As such, there is often concern expressed when discussion about making changes begins. Some feel that what was good enough for them is good enough for the children of today; others may feel uncomfortable with an educational setting that is not in a traditional classroom.

Because of this, when making a transition of an educational model, it is wise to have a small group of people working together in the process. Identify individuals who have a passion for Sunday School or VBS, past and present. This may include former teachers, parents, new teachers, or individuals who have children's ministry experience from another congregation.

Be clear about your expectations as you ask people to be a part of your team. If your goal is to make the transition to a new style of Sunday School or VBS, share this information with individuals up front. Be sure that you also share with these individuals why you feel they would be an asset to the task.

Let people know the approximate time frame for the team task and how you will identify when their task is completed. As you share your vision—and include a variety of people in the transition process—your volunteers will develop a sense of ownership in the project as they help build support for the change.

Identify the Purpose for Rotation

One of the first tasks of your team will be to identify why you are making the shift to a rotation model for Sunday School or VBS. What are your goals and outcomes for children's ministry? How will a rotation model help you to achieve those goals?

Some goals for Sunday School or VBS may seem to be common sense, such as for children to learn about the Bible and grow in their faith, but individuals might have other reasons for wanting to see a successful children's ministry program.

At one of your early team meetings, have each member write down their ideas concerning what they would like to see accomplished through Sunday School. In a large group, list all of these individual goals. Next to the goal, identify how a rotation model Sunday School or VBS could help achieve that particular goal differently from your current model. If there are goals listed that cannot be accomplished through a rotation model, talk about what needs to happen to achieve these goals.

Through this exercise, your team should begin to identify the reasoning behind the style of rotation program you plan to offer. Additionally, team members will be able to articulate these decisions to others.

Lessons Learned

Before you begin any change in the structure of Sunday School or Vacation Bible School, make sure your pastor supports exploring the transition. While boards or committees may not support every idea presented, it is also important to have their "blessing" as you begin this process.

Identify Your Rotation Format

One of the unique advantages of rotation Sunday School or VBS is that there are many variations possible under any one technique or style of rotation. In subsequent chapters, you will read about the different ways to incorporate rotation into Sunday School and VBS. Before moving ahead in your transition, your team will need to identify what format works best for you.

Assist team members as they study the different styles of rotation. Compare these models with the goals and outcomes you've already identified. Discuss the pros and cons of each format and how it will work for your setting. In some cases, more than one format may work for your congregation. Your team's task is to answer the question of which model will work best for your congregation and needs.

Identify Facility and Resource Options

At the same time your team is identifying the preferred rotation format, you will need to consider the space allocation for your program. Are you using shared space or is it exclusively for Sunday School, VBS, and other children's programs? If you are sharing space, with whom are you sharing it? How often and in what ways does each agency use the space?

Besides space, what other resources do you have at your disposal? Do you have computers for a computer lab or a bus to take a group off-site for a learning experience? Do you have a large room for movie projection or multiple sets of audio visual equipment, if needed? Is there a space available for cooking or something that could be easily modified?

Compare your space and resources with the different rotation formats. If you are going to be using a shared space, this is the time to add everyone who uses that space to the discussion. This way, you can evaluate the feasibility of using a particular format.

Oftentimes, at this stage of your planning, it becomes easy to see the difficulties in making the transition to rotation, instead of the blessings. Challenges with shared space or other issues frequently become perceived as obstacles to rotation models because of the configuration of activities and larger groups. Don't get discouraged! Always go back to your initial goals and objectives and see how you can accomplish them.

Be creative in your thinking! For example, you may want a cooking workshop but the church kitchen is already in use on Sunday mornings or is in a location that isn't conducive to children. Many cooking activities can be accomplished with a microwave and/or a large toaster oven. Do you have a space that you can use these that is easier for children and your program?

If you are looking at shared space where materials cannot be kept out during the week, consider purchasing crates on wheels that can be stored in one place and easily brought out when needed.

Curriculum

Once you have identified your goals and purpose, rotation format, and how you will use your facility, the next step in making your transition is selecting your curriculum.

The popularity of the rotation format for Sunday School and Vacation Bible School is growing. As a result, new curriculums are being published as well. Check with your local Christian bookstore and preferred publishing company for recommendations they might have. Traditional Sunday School curriculums can also be adapted to fit your rotation needs, especially if the curriculum is designed to have multiple classes studying the same story at the same time.

> **Lessons Learned**
>
> Concordia Publishing House's VBS curriculum is written using a rotation model. For details on converting CPH's Growing in Christ Sunday School to a rotation model, see chapter 8.

As you select your curriculum, it is important that you once again go back to your goals and purpose for Sunday School or VBS. Review the curriculum to see if it fits with your goals and objectives. Also, before you select your curriculum, identify what adaptations, if any, need to happen to fit your circumstances and who might be able to do them.

Staffing Needs

Once your format and curriculum are selected and you've identified your space, you are ready to begin staffing your new Sunday School or VBS! How exciting! As you communicate and talk with people, be sure to share why you are making the changes, and how you see this as a positive step in the faith formation of the children of your congregation. Help others catch the vision and be excited about being a part of this important ministry!

Your rotation format will assist in determining the staff you will need. In addition to having your Shepherds and Teacher/Presenters, it is also helpful to have support staff throughout the year. These individuals assist in areas such as attendance, missions, setup and takedown, supply coordination, and curriculum development. The more people you have involved with the program, the more ownership there will be and excitement as it moves to fruition.

Communication

When making any changes in the church, it is always important to communicate, communicate, communicate! Regularly update staff members and the sponsoring board or group for your Sunday School or VBS on the steps and direction the ministry is going. Confirm the support of the pastor, communicating why the changes are taking place. Be sure to give regular updates to parents, so that they also understand why the changes are being made. Use a variety of ways to communicate—both verbally and in writing.

The Transition

Creating a new or adapted environment for children to learn about the love of Christ is a very exciting endeavor. It is a lot of work, and initially will involve many people supporting and giving direction to make it happen. But on the first Sunday when children come to a new way of "doing" Sunday School—and later when older students ask, "Why didn't you do that when I was in Sunday School?"—you will realize the fruits of the labor and how involved children and adults alike will become.

3

Large Group/ Small Group

By Leah Abel

Question: What Sunday School program guarantees that children look forward to Sunday School all week, every student learning need is addressed, parents are always appreciative, and volunteers are beating down the door to get involved with the program?

Answer: None! That Sunday School program doesn't exist. But that doesn't mean it's time to give up. Through perseverance and some open-minded creativity, our Sunday School has been transformed from a sedentary classroom to a dynamic interactive space that has been well received by participants and staff.

Many Sunday School leaders have searched diligently for the perfect Sunday School curriculum and format only to be left frustrated. Our church is no exception. Like many of you, we have often been more aware of our shortcomings than our victories. We have shaken our heads and pointed fingers but have often found ourselves short on solutions. We have asked for feedback only to be discouraged when it yielded more questions than answers. We have struggled to find just the right fit for Sunday mornings, one to best meet the needs of children, families, and volunteers while effectively communicating God's Word in a clear, life-shaping way.

As we have worked over the years to make our Sunday School ministry more effective, our biggest struggle has been helping teachers, both new and experienced, change the way they think about the teaching task. It seemed like no matter how much time we spent at training events and monthly meetings saying that we wanted teachers to have the kids up and moving and interacting with the material (using the games, active storytelling, conversation, etc.), they continued to teach with the only model they really knew: kids sitting in desks or at tables, listening while teachers talk, then doing a worksheet, coloring sheet, or a punch-out/sticker craft. It's the model they remember from their school days and the model of their own Sunday School experience.

After attempts to improve teacher training for three consecutive years failed to produce the results we were looking for, we decided to head in a new direction. We decided to make significant changes to the look of Sunday School in order to change the thinking of our teachers. Rather than make a few small changes and hope for the best, we presented teachers and students with a radically different experience. We knew change would be hard on all of us, and we expected some questions and opposition. But it was time for a change. We didn't want to settle for a less than exceptional program for our children. We chose a large-group, small-group model.

The concept is fairly simple. Children spend time in a small group with a single leader and then transition to a large group for a time of music and learning. Following the large-group event, children travel back to their small groups for processing and application. This format provided us with an opportunity to model the kind of active learning and creative teaching that we had been encouraging our teachers to attempt in their traditional classroom settings. It also gave them the tools they needed to make it happen without additional time and effort.

How It Works

As children arrive, parents take them to their designated small-group area where they are greeted by their small-group leader. Small-group leaders welcome the children, take attendance, and dive in to the warm-up activity. These activities help introduce the Bible point for the day and prepare the children for what they will see and hear during the large-group presentation. Activities range from question and answer discussions to simple games. This time lasts for 15–20 minutes.

When small-group leaders and children hear the music start playing, that is their signal to wrap up their activity and discussion and move to the front of the room for large-group time.

Large-group time begins with a song or two (this allows groups that have not completed their activity to finish up) and then the Bible lesson is presented by the large-group team using videos, puppets, skits, and object lessons. The media used varies from week to week, but consistent song leaders and story presenters help establish continuity in routine and expectation for the children.

Small-group leaders guide their children to the large-group area and provide any needed assistance. After the large-group presentation, children return with their leaders to their small-group area for lesson application. This small-group time is extremely valuable for small-group leaders to ensure the children understood the Bible story, the Bible point of the week, and the application that it can have to their lives. This time may include a craft, an activity, or even a snack that helps to reinforce the lesson.

At the end of the Sunday School hour, parents come back to meet their children and sign them out with the small-group leader.

Lessons Learned

With a large space, small groups do not have their own doors. Sometimes this causes confusion for parents trying to determine whether or not it is the appropriate time to come in and pick up their child. To help reduce distractions, the gym doors are closed during the Sunday School hour. We have a sign on the door informing parents that the doors will be opened at the end of the lesson.

The Team

Small-group leaders are the primary caregivers for children. They are responsible for a small group of eight to ten children. Upon arriving, the leaders gather supplies, greet parents and children, lead opening activities and questions, take children to and from the large-group event, and lead their small group

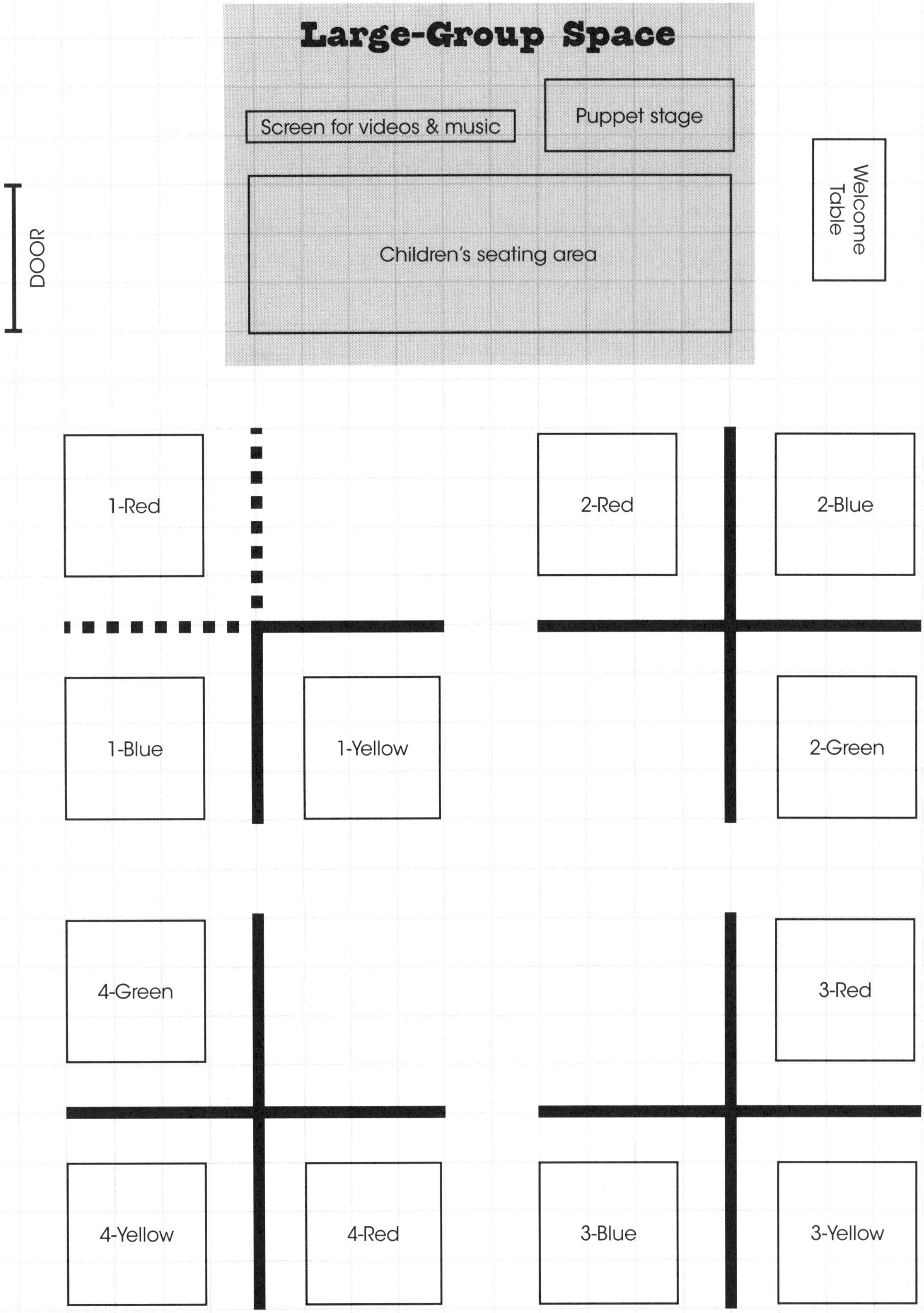
Large-Group Space
Screen for videos & music
Puppet stage
Children's seating area
Welcome Table
DOOR
DOOR
1-Red
2-Red
2-Blue
1-Blue
1-Yellow
2-Green
4-Green
3-Red
4-Yellow
4-Red
3-Blue
3-Yellow

in the closing activity. Since preparation is minimal, teachers are encouraged to focus their energy on the relationship aspects within the small group.

The large-group presentation team includes an emcee, actors and actresses, puppeteers, and song leaders. We have had fantastic results involving high school students in this part of the program. They enjoy the responsibility and the opportunity to ham it up in front of the children. Our group meets monthly to plan out the coming month. An "expert teacher" who is energetic, experienced with crowd control, creative, and loves kids is an ideal candidate for the role of emcee and group leader.

We also incorporate a supply coordinator. This person prepares the supplies for each week's lessons. The supplies are then waiting for the small-group leaders to pick up when they arrive.

Lessons Learned

Don't undersell the small-group leader commitment level. The preparation time for the small-group leaders is much less than that of traditional teachers, which is a big selling point with volunteers, and small-group leaders don't need to worry about gathering supplies or even leading the Bible story. Volunteers, however, need to commit to being consistent leaders for the children in their group. This leads to more consistent attendance by group members. Stress the importance of building relationships with the children in their groups.

The Space

Space was a primary concern for us when we first considered this model. The only large space available to us is our school gym (which we now transform every Sunday into the Sunday School center, see diagram on page 16). We needed spaces for twelve small groups and our priorities included ease of setup, limiting distractions for groups, and easy access to the large-group space. In order to meet those needs, we purchased eight collapsible, wheeled dividers and a blanket for each group. To create the "classrooms," the dividers are folded at 90 degree angles and placed corner to corner. (Dashed line on the diagram represents one folded divider.)

Each small group gets two walls for meeting space. This has proven to be adequate in reducing the distractions that watching other groups can provide. The walls also provide a place for leaders to hang attendance charts and coloring sheets or art projects if they would like.

Large-group time takes place in the front of the room. A puppet stage and screen for videos and song lyrics take center stage. Children generally sit on the floor with teachers on small chairs behind them.

Transforming the space is a weekly routine for us now. Our setup schedule looks like this:

7:15–7:30 a.m.—Gym floor is covered. (We cover the gym floor to prevent damage by dress shoes, glue, glitter, etc.)

7:30–7:45 a.m.—Puppet stage is assembled and dividers are set out in their places.

7:45–8:00 a.m.—Supply bins are placed in the front of the room and blankets are set out in each "classroom."

8:00–9:00 a.m.—Volunteers attend worship.

9:00–9:15 a.m.—Large-group team assembles for prayer and last minute preparations.

9:15 a.m.—Small-group leaders arrive; one to two members of the large-group team staff the welcome table.

9:30 a.m.—Sunday School begins!

Setup is typically performed by three people and has proven to be a great way to involve people who might not otherwise get involved with Christian education. Teardown is usually done in 30 minutes as teachers, students, and parents help to fold up dividers and blankets.

Lessons Learned

Chairs or no chairs? Setup and teardown of a blanket for each small group is significantly easier than chairs for each group. However, some of our small-group leaders felt that chairs helped their students to better focus. Our solution: chairs are stacked in a corner of the gym. Leaders wishing to utilize the chairs arrive early and grab just enough for their group.

Forming Small Groups

Our groups are grade specific, which allows small-group leaders to gear their discussions to the reading and learning levels of the children. The ideal is to have small groups of eight to ten children on a given Sunday. When groups are formed at the beginning of the year, we assign fifteen to eighteen children to each group, understanding that children will likely not attend every week. At our larger campus, we have multiple groups for each grade level. These groups are designated by grade and color: 2nd red, 2nd blue, 4th yellow, 1st green, and so forth.

How do we decide who goes in which small group? We have a Rally Day celebration prior to the first week of class where students register for their grade level. Our leaders meet during the following week to divide the children into groups, being sure to be sensitive to small-group leader requests and student needs of which they are aware. When students come back for the first week of classes, their groups are posted on the doors and in the large-group space. Greeters and large-group leaders help students find their group and meet their small-group leader on the first Sunday.

Lessons Learned

One challenge with multiple groups in one large space is assuring that parents and their children can easily find the appropriate small group for their child. A welcome table by the main door assists parents in finding their child's group. Children and parents will get used to the routine, but the greeter role is key during the first few weeks for producing a safe, positive environment.

The Right Curriculum for the Right Students

Students in the lower grades (first through fourth) are hearing and learning the same lesson each week in the same space. The curriculum studies both Old and New Testament Bible stories. Small-group leaders focus on relationships and faith conversation to aid children in applying the story to their own lives and seeing how the Gospel works in their lives. Because our small groups are grade specific, the small-group leaders can speak with their groups in an age-appropriate way.

Our older elementary students (grades five and six) meet separately using a different curriculum than the younger children. They use the small-group/large-group model, but with one minor difference: their large-group time is not led by a separate team. Instead, the various small groups participate in leading the large-group time. The group assigned to that week may prepare during the initial 20 minutes of small-group time, then participate in large-group time, and finally return to their small group at the end for application and processing just as in the younger grades.

Younger children, in preschool and kindergarten, do not participate in the small-group/large-group model. Instead, they meet in self-contained classrooms to ensure comfort in a routine, limiting the confusion of changing locations or teachers.

Supplies

Each small-group leader has his or her own supply bin that contains specific items for the week's lesson. The bin is also used to store standard items like crayons, pencils, kid-size scissors, and glue sticks. The bin may also be used by the leader to store odds and ends that are used when the class finishes the discussion early, such as Bible trivia cards, extra coloring sheets, stickers, prizes, and so forth.

What We Love about This Model

Our leaders have exhibited change in their understanding of the teaching task. They have realized their primary task is not to simply read sentences from a book or lead craft activities, but to form relationships with children and help them understand and apply God's Word to their lives. Because the primary Bible teaching task is handled by the large-group team, small-group leaders are allowed to keep their focus on those relationships, thus making greater connections. This focus on relationships has made it easier to bring in young and inexperienced teachers and high school assistants to serve as small-group leaders. Some of the young teachers and assistants have received rave reviews by both parents and kids alike for showing it can be "cool to be Christian."

A Smaller Church Twist

Our congregation has recently established a second worship location. On Sunday mornings, we have a large worshiping community that meets on our original campus and a smaller, growing group that currently meets at a local elementary school for worship and Sunday School. This has allowed us to experience the small-group/large-group model with two different-size worshiping communities. Our main campus has an average attendance of one hundred plus students while our new location has an average attendance of ten to fifteen children.

At the new location, the format for the morning, supply needs, and Bible lessons remain the same. This consistency streamlines the process and makes Sunday School manageable for the mission congregation, which often has other issues related to using a rented facility. Small-group time is first, followed by the large-group presentation (puppets, videos, object lessons, etc.). The session ends with more small-group time. However, there are a few alterations that we have made to better meet the needs of the community. First, small groups are not grade specific. With lower numbers, these small groups are able to be more flexible. With attendance of ten to fifteen children, ten students may meet together as a single small group, or fifteen students may be divided into two groups of seven and eight. Second, music time takes place at the beginning while children are assembling. This time also allows leaders to ascertain how many groups will be ideal for a given morning. Finally, the large-group presentation team is smaller. We alter the large-group skits to be sure they can be performed by two to three people.

The large-group presentation component has provided an excellent venue to model various teaching methods. One of the decisions we made was to make sure we had the right people in place as the large-group presentation leaders. We took our most animated, active, creative teachers and put them in the emcee roles. This has made a huge difference in the way kids engage with the lessons. It has also opened the eyes of teachers to new ways of communicating God's Word.

For years we have fought the "Sunday School feels too much like school" battle, particularly with those families whose children attend our Christian Day School. Switching to this model has allowed us to move children out of the school building where many of them attend classes during the week, thus changing the "feel." The lessons do not look or feel like those they have in the classroom during the week. Our small-group focus combined with large-group storytelling has helped us address more effectively the biblical literacy difference between those students that attend our Day School and those who do not. The creative teaching presentation takes children beyond observing the lesson and moves them toward experiencing the lesson as a group. Children experience the story together and then spend time unpacking it. This curbs the tendency of students who have learned the content before to answer questions before other students have a chance to connect with the story.

We're making progress. We have not seen our numbers skyrocket, but we have seen a change in understanding of the teaching task by teachers. We have gained more new teachers. Among our children, we have also seen a greater level of connection between the story and their lives. Furthermore, we are able to deal more effectively with the biblical literacy difference between those students that attend our Day School and those who do not.

Although we are still in the beginning stages of this new model, preliminary feedback from participants and staff looks great. The change has been worth the investment of time and energy, and we anticipate continued growth in this dynamic ministry.

4

Site Rotation

By Scott Rauch

Take Another Look

So what does the Teacher Guide want me to do this week? Let's see. It says I should be offering a creative mix of worship, music, reading of the Bible, life application, a craft, and a closing prayer. That's a lot to get into a one-hour time period. That's a lot of creativity from one person. That's a lot of planning and preparation and gathering of supplies and time.

Really, if you think about it, for many Sunday School classrooms these various curricular pieces take place on a weekly basis. It even happens pretty well at times. God uses the gifts of maybe one or two adults in a classroom to see that the story of His love in Jesus Christ is taught faithfully. But it is a lot of work for a few people. What if you could spread those gifts out through more people, some of whom may have specific skills or interests in leading a particular part of the curriculum?

That's where site rotation comes in. Simply put, site rotation takes the pieces of a specific lesson from a Sunday School or Vacation Bible School out of one room and splits them into different sites or locations. It is an opportunity for adults to be involved in the Christian education of children in areas more conducive to their interests, talents, and abilities.

Getting Started

Let's take a look at the typical pieces of a Sunday School and see how different sites might work for a one-hour time period. Remember that we are not tampering with the teaching of the Bible, rather we are allowing for the unique gifts and talents of God's people to flow forth in a creative educational manner with children. Various pieces might include an opening and/or closing worship time, Bible story/life-application time, music time, crafts time, library time, refreshment time, game time, or other creative opportunities for children to learn in the best ways possible. Let's take a look at what might happen at some of these sites. Suggested schedules are included at the end of this chapter.

A site-rotation model could begin (and/or end) with a weekly time for children and adults to gather together for a brief devotional worship time geared for their age level. That means that early childhood and elementary age children probably need unique and/or separate worship times with creative music, prayers, and age-appropriate messages that can be used to lead children in their worship of the Lord.

A brief devotional time might include

- the invocation, which helps children to remember that all that we do begins in God's name;
- a song, hymn, or perhaps even a piece of the worship liturgy so that children continue to learn this important aspect of a congregations' primary worship service;
- a brief thought on the theme of the day as drawn out of the curriculum;
- an offering gathered and a reminder of what the offering is being used for;
- a time of prayer, including the Lord's Prayer; and
- a benediction, which helps children know they are blessed by the Lord in all ways.

This devotional/worship time could be held in a larger area or even the church sanctuary. This is an opportunity for adults, or even older youth, to provide leadership with music, the liturgy, and presentation of the message. From this starting point, the children separate out to various sites for the rest of the Sunday School time.

Site Specifics

One of the top organizational priorities is assigning areas or rooms for creative presentation of the weekly Bible story. This same area may include discussion of how the theme or message of the story applies to the students' lives. Brainstorm all the possibilities within your church building and grounds. In some cases, your storytelling site might be a designated room is used regularly. Depending on theme of the story, or even the physical elements of the story, the leader/storyteller might choose another location inside or outside of the church to help with their creative presentation. The leaders might choose to meet in the kitchen for a look at the Passover. A dark closet with its tight fit might be good for a discussion of how sin impacts our lives in uncomfortable ways. Even taking a walk and having a conversation like Jesus did with His disciples is an idea worth exploring. The sites choices are limited only by what is considered appropriate use (and appropriate permissions) and the creativity of the teacher/storyteller.

Giving children time to work with art is always helpful, but it can provide a challenge to many adults. Children need to have opportunities to create hands-on pieces of art that apply to the theme of the day. Here is a great opportunity for someone who loves art to help develop or manage age-appropriate craft projects and provide leadership with the teacher of a particular class or maybe even a couple of classes together. A crafts leader or team should have a designated area or room where all the art supplies are located. Classes then visit the art room on a regular basis, whether weekly or monthly, depending on the time needed for an art project.

Leading children in singing about their faith in God can be a powerful part of a site-rotation Sunday School. Youth or adult leaders can help children learn age-appropriate songs, whether as a formal choir or just as an opportunity for singing together. While some churches have a music or choir rehearsal room, almost every church has a sanctuary with at least a piano available for use. A music site also provides opportunities for children to share their musical gifts. Think about the great gift children can give to a class or the church with music.

While many congregations may not have a library, the possibility of gathering a variety of appropriate books for children to read themselves or to have read to them is an idea that any size church can explore. Providing them solid Christian reading materials is a great gift to children. Having someone manage a shelf of books or an entire room of books is a great opportunity for an individual, or even a team of people, who may not want to teach an entire class but would be willing to help organize a small library. A class might visit the library area on a regular basis, check books out to take home, or have a book read to them.

One area we usually hesitate to consider, often due to time or location concerns, is a game area for children. Play, whether organized or free, is an important way for children to grow in their Christian friendships. Games can be used to help affirm a specific part of a lesson. Games might be active or quiet. And they can be oriented for the individual, provide competition between groups of children, or a give an entire group of children a challenge to accomplish. A Sunday School does not have to have a bunch of sports equipment to play games with children. They also do not have to have a designated area or room for games. Games can be played in a hallway or outside, depending on the circumstances. Think of the learning that can happen as children are guided in their play or are given opportunities to have some fun together with their Christian friends.

Fitting It All In

So how does one get all this done in one hour? Most curriculums intentionally provide more activities than can be done in a single Sunday School hour. Teachers can pick and choose what works best for them and the children in their class.

A site-rotation model can work much the same way. A Sunday School might design their rotation based on the strengths in their congregation. Leaders work with their youth and adults to determine how best to use their facility. A site-rotation model can be used from week to week or on a monthly schedule. You could interchange various parts from week to week. Games, library, and crafts could be set up for classes to rotate through on a monthly basis. However, it is important to have a regular schedule developed for the Sunday School.

Site rotation helps a Sunday School that needs to creatively adjust its regular ministry without sacrificing the regular

Lessons Learned

No one rotation model works for every church and size. Work with the gifts and talents God provides in your congregation. Small churches also face special concerns. See chapter 7 for more details.

pieces of teaching. It can be operated in any size Sunday School. In fact, site rotation may provide a creative option for the small Sunday School, one that is sometimes overlooked. Small Sunday Schools often struggle to find adults to serve as teachers. But with a site-rotation model, adults with talents in areas other than the direct week-to-week teaching can be used to help operate the Sunday School. What a great way for a church to provide a good teaching experience for children so that their faith in Jesus is nurtured through the study of God's Word.

Ready to Go

So, I'm looking at my Teacher Guide again, and suddenly it hits me. I e-mail my Sunday School Superintendent and ask if we could begin collecting books to create a children's library. I then call the church organist to see if there are people in the congregation who could help my children learn some songs every other week. And then I send a text message to that high school junior who is a fantastic artist and see if we can work together to create an arts and crafts closet. Then I can really focus on telling the Bible story in the best creative ways I can and have the energy and time to do it well. It may take some time to get all this set up, but it could work. Let's give it a try!

Here are three possible site-rotation schedules that can be used as a starting point in developing your model.

Schedule 1 – Weekly Site Rotation

9:30–9:40	Opening Devotion	Kindergarten–Grade 6	Gym
	Opening Devotion	Three- to four-year-olds	Classroom
9:40–9:55	Bible Story Teaching Time	Three-year-olds–Grade 6	Classrooms
9:55–10:10	Craft Time	Three- to four-year-olds	Art Room
	Music Time	Kindergarten–Grade 6	Sanctuary
10:10–10:25	Craft Time	Kindergarten–Grade 6	Art Room
	Music Time	Three- to four-year-olds	Sanctuary
10:25–10:30	Closing Prayer	Three-year-olds–Grade 6	Classrooms

Schedule 2 – Two-Sunday Site Rotation

First Sunday

9:00–9:15	Opening Worship	Grades 1–6	Sanctuary
	Opening Worship	Three-year-olds–Kind.	Gym
9:15–9:35	Bible Story Teaching Time	Three-year-olds–Grade 6	Classrooms
9:35–9:55	Craft Time	Grades 1–6	Craft Area
	Library Reading Time	Three-year-olds–Kind.	Library
9:55–10:00	Closing Prayer	Three-year-olds–Grade 6	Classrooms

Second Sunday

9:00–9:15	Opening Worship	Grades 1–6	Sanctuary
	Opening Worship	Three-year-olds–Kind.	Gym
9:15–9:35	Bible Story Teaching Time	Three-year-olds–Grade 6	Classrooms
9:35–9:55	Game Time	Grades 4–6	Gym
	Music Time	Grades 1–3	Sanctuary
	Craft Time	Three-year-olds–Kind.	Craft Area
9:55–10:00	Closing Prayer	Three-year-olds–Grade 6	Classrooms

Schedule 3 – Four-Sunday Site Rotation

First Sunday

9:15–9:30	Opening Worship	Grades 1–6	Parish Hall
	Opening Worship	Three-year-olds–Kind.	Kind. Room
9:30–9:50	Bible Story Teaching Time	Three-year-olds–Grade 3	Classrooms
9:30–10:10	Bible Story Teaching Time	Grades 4–6	Classrooms
9:50–10:10	Craft Time	Grades 1–3	Craft Area
9:50–10:00	Library Time	Three-year-olds–Kind.	Library
10:00–10:10	Refreshments	Three-year-olds–Kind.	Parish Hall
10:10–10:15	Closing Worship	Three-year-olds–Grade 6	Classrooms

Second Sunday

9:15–9:30	Opening Worship	Grades 1–6	Parish Hall
	Opening Worship	Three-year-olds–Kind.	Kind. Room
9:30–9:50	Bible Story Teaching Time	Three-year-olds–Grade 6	Classrooms
9:50–10:10	Game Time	Grades 1–3	Playground
	Craft Time	Grades 4–6	Craft Area
9:50–10:00	Music Time	Three-year-olds–Kind.	Sanctuary
10:00–10:10	Refreshments	Three-year-olds–Kind.	Parish Hall
10:10–10:15	Closing Worship	Three-year-olds–Grade 6	Classrooms

Third Sunday

9:15–9:30	Opening Worship	Grades 1–6	Parish Hall
	Opening Worship	Three-year-olds–Kind.	Kind. Room
9:30–9:50	Bible Story Teaching Time	Three-year-olds–Grade 6	Classrooms

9:50–10:10	Library Time	Grades 1–3	Library
	Music Time	Grades 4–6	Sanctuary
9:50–10:00	Game Time	Three-year-olds–Kind.	Playground
10:00–10:10	Refreshments	Three-year-olds–Kind.	Parish Hall
10:10–10:15	Closing Worship	Three-year-olds–Grade 6	Classrooms
Fourth Sunday			
9:15–9:30	Opening Worship	Grades 1–6	Parish Hall
	Opening Worship	Three-year-olds–Kind.	Kind. Room
9:30–9:50	Bible Story Teaching Time	Three-year-olds–Grade 6	Classrooms
9:30–10:10	Bible Story Teaching Time	Grades 4–6	Classrooms
9:50–10:10	Game Time	Grades 1–3	Playground
9:50–10:00	Craft Time	Three-year-olds–Kind.	Craft Area
10:00–10:10	Refreshments	Three-year-olds–Kind.	Parish Hall
10:10–10:15	Closing Worship	Three-year-olds–Grade 6	Classrooms

5

Modified Rotation

By Kathleen Lane

Our Sunday School leaders addressed several issues when making plans for changes for our middle and upper grade Sunday School classes. We recognized the need to build excitement, offer a broader variety of experiences, and get students more actively involved in learning activities. A rotation format seemed to be the answer, but we had some reservations. We had a large enrollment with limited space for large groups. There were concerns about large-group management and the time wasted moving and getting settled into each activity. We also had a dedicated group of teachers who enjoyed getting to know their own students. These teachers were skilled at relating Bible truths and excited about sharing their faith in a small-group setting. A modified rotation format seemed to be the best fit for the space and leader interests/skills available.

In this modified rotation format, classroom teachers or a substitute are with their own group each week and still do most of the lesson planning and presentation. Other leaders with special interests (and usually limitations on their volunteer time) develop plans for additional, more active learning experiences. Each of these special activities is offered to individual classes two to four times during the school year, usually in their own classroom. For the occasional sessions when a multi-class activity is held, lower grade groups are shuffled so that larger space is available for the Grade 3–6 students. Except for music, each activity takes up the whole class period.

The Rotation Activities

Bible Story

Classroom teachers present and discuss the Bible story with their own assigned small group of students in their own classroom. Lesson materials from Growing in Christ are used, but the schedule is modified so the Bible lessons are not always covered on the dates noted on the materials. Extra communication and training is given so that teachers know how to use the Church Year information incorporated with the materials at the right time, not necessarily on the day the lesson is taught. Knowing that games and crafts will be done during specified sessions, teachers might choose not to do those activities during their regular lesson.

Music

Music is used to praise God, learn Bible verses, pray, and reinforce Bible truths. The students prepare songs to be sung during worship services two to three times during the school year. Music from Growing in Christ, past VBS material, and other contemporary music sources is used. CDs and DVDs work especially well as accompaniment for a large group of students. All students gather together for half of a session once each month for music.

Computer Room

Each class rotates to the computer room three to four times during the year. Students use software that relates to the Bible stories being discussed in the classrooms or that reviews general Bible facts and concepts. Resources found at www.sundaysoftware.com are great additions to the curriculum. For instance, lesson plans developed from the *Exodus Adventures* program can be used during the quarter when Moses Bible stories are taught. *Galilee Flyer* is a good resource when the curriculum includes Jesus' parables and the Lord's Prayer.

Bible Review Games

Students play games to review recently covered material as well as general Bible knowledge. Game sessions are offered to each class two to three times per year. The Bible Review Cards from Growing in Christ

Lessons Learned

No one model works in every situation. Consider a number of strategies and approaches until you find the one that works for your situation.

materials are a valuable resource for these games as are the ideas given in the resource pages of the Teacher Guide.

Crafts

Craft projects are completed by each class twice a year. Since a whole session is devoted to this, more lasting and meaningful crafts can be done. Craft projects are tied into the Bible lesson or the time of the Church Year. Ideas for crafts are found in the Growing in Christ Teacher Guides, in the many craft books available from Concordia Publishing House (www.cph.org), and at local hobby stores. Each craft session includes a short devotion or faith discussion related to the craft.

Family Festivals

Parents and grandparents are invited to join students twice a year for a variety of family learning experiences. These festivals include all grade 3–6 students on the same day. Some sessions have the whole group together for singing, puppet shows, drama, or talent shows. Occasionally, a Family Festival will be presented by a traveling Christian musician, district camp personnel, or local clowning troupe. Other times, the group might be split up to rotate among three to four different activities such as games, family discussion, or crafts.

Mission/Service Activities

All classes participate in these mission activities on the same days, two to three times a year. Students learn about the work of missionaries, pray for missionaries, learn how they can be in mission, and are involved in some hands-on projects. Materials are developed using the ideas and resources available from LCMS World Mission (mission.lcms.org) or Concordia Publishing House's Sunday School Web site (sundayschool.cph.org). The *Mission Friends* publications are great resources. Hands-on projects have included assembling school supply or hygiene kits for the local shelter, making VBS craft kits to be used by servant teams in Mexico, making bookmarks for Bibles being sent to Sudan, or making valentines for members of the armed forces. If available, a missionary or servant team member might relate his or her experiences to the whole group.

The Rotation Schedule

A ten-week schedule for our modified rotation format might look like this:

Date	Class 1	Class 2	Class 3	Class 4
Date	Lesson 1/Music	Lesson 1/Music	Lesson 1/Music	Lesson 1/Music
Date	Lesson 2	Lesson 2	Lesson 2	Lesson 2
Date	Craft or Games	Craft or Games	Craft or Games	Lesson 3
Date	Lesson 3	Lesson 3	Lesson 3	Lesson 4
Date	Lesson 4/Music	Lesson 4/Music	Lesson 4/Music	Lesson 5/Music
Date	Lesson 5	Lesson 5	Lesson 5	Compter Lab
Date	Lesson 6	Lesson 6	Lesson 6	Craft or Games
Date	Lesson 7	Computer Lab	Computer Lab	Lesson 6
Date	Computer Lab/Music	Lesson 7/Music	Lesson 7/Music	Lesson 7/Music
Date	Family Fest/Missions	Family Fest/Missions	Family Fest/Missions	Family Fest/Missions

Class 5	Class 6	Class 7	Class 8	Class 9
Lesson 1/Music	Lesson 1/Music	Lesson 1/Music	Lesson 1/Music	Computer Lab/Music
Lesson 2	Lesson 2	Lesson 2	Computer Lab	Lesson 1
Lesson 3	Lesson 3	Computer Lab	Lesson 2	Lesson 2s
Lesson 4	Computer Lab	Craft or Games	Craft or Games	Craft or Games
Computer Lab/Music	Lesson 4/Music	Lesson 3/Music	Lesson 3/Music	Lesson 3/Music
Lesson 5	Lesson 5	Lesson 4	Lesson 4	Lesson 4
Craft or Games	Craft or Games	Lesson 5	Lesson 5	Lesson 5
Lesson 6	Lesson 6	Lesson 6	Lesson 6	Lesson 6
Lesson 7/Music	Lesson 7/Music	Lesson 7/Music	Lesson 7/Music	Lesson 7/Music
Family Fest/Missions	Family Fest/Missions	Family Fest/Missions	Family Fest/Missions	Family Fest/Missions

The Staff

Classroom Teachers

These teachers are most involved with the students. They plan and present the weekly Bible lessons to their small group of students. They also are with the class when other activities are offered, helping to supervise and give aid as needed. One teacher is responsible for a group of eight to ten students. Teachers may choose to team teach a class, and they may choose to teach for a half or whole year.

Music Leaders

This staff person selects and leads appropriate hymns and songs. He or she also procures the needed accompaniment, whether live or recorded, and coordinates the group's musical offerings during worship services. One leader is adequate for this once-a-month activity.

Computer Room Leaders

Computer Leaders are responsible for researching available resources, recommending purchases, and maintaining computer equipment and software. They develop lesson plans and lead the students in the computer-based activities. One to three leaders are needed, with one of them present at each session.

Game Leaders

Game Leaders develop Bible review games, obtain all needed supplies, and lead the students in playing the games. One leader is needed for each class playing games on any given day. These leaders work with students for about six sessions throughout the year.

Craft Leaders

Craft Leaders come up with craft ideas, procure all the supplies, and instruct the students in completing their crafts. They also develop a devotion or faith discussion related to the project. At least one leader is needed for each class doing crafts on any given day. They work with students for about six sessions throughout the year.

Family Festival Leaders

The Sunday School Superintendent, Leadership Team, and Director of Christian Education (DCE) make the plans for Family Festival activities. Other leaders are recruited as necessary to lead singing, crafts, games, and other activities.

Mission Activities Leaders

The Sunday School Superintendent, Leadership Team, and DCE make the plans for mission activities and projects. They develop the lesson plan and obtain the materials, which are then given to classroom teachers to use with their own students. Other volunteer leaders might be recruited to help with the projects.

The Blessings of Modified Rotation

This modified rotation format has been a good fit for our present situation. Modified rotation has brought new excitement and energy to our Sunday School. We've seen the greatest impact in four areas.

- Our Classroom Teachers are still able to do what they do best. They are freed from the time-consuming preparation of games and crafts so that they can research the Bible story and then lead their students in meaningful, small-group Bible study. Since they see their students on a weekly basis, they are able to build strong relationships with their students and families.
- More people are involved in our Sunday School program. Those unable to commit to a whole semester of teaching are still able to use their talents by occasionally leading games, crafts, and so forth.
- Our Family Festivals bring parents and children together for faith-building activities. This has resulted in the parents being more connected to Sunday School. They have even been inspired to use some of the Family Festival activities as models for their own family devotions.
- Students are excited about the variety of learning experiences offered. We hear statements like "I've got to be here next week. It's our turn to be in the Computer Lab" and "Can I bring my friend next week when we make crafts?"

As you consider the needs for your Sunday School, think about how your congregation may benefit from a modified rotation Sunday School.

Workshop Rotation

By Chris Schomburg

Introduction

Are you stimulated to learn while sitting face-forward in a hard plastic chair, still next to the person who irritates you most in the world, in the same boring classroom where you've already memorized the number of ceiling tiles, the location of every piece of tape-peeled paint mark, where you have been told "sit still and listen!" for the thousandth time by the same teacher you didn't like in September and you don't like any more in March, while hearing about a single subject for an hour?

Now do it again the next week . . . and the next week . . . and the next week. . . . *Ad infinitum*. Are you eager to learn more? to come back? Even if what you are learning about is the greatest subject in the world for all time—and, of course, the topic of our Savior's love for us *is* the greatest subject in the world—if our learning environment is not stimulating, we will not only be less likely to enjoy being there, but we will also be less likely to retain the information we have been taught.

Newsflash! The world has changed! Sunday School was a great idea when it began in the late 1700s in England, where poor people were taught how to read and write on Sundays, using the Bible as a textbook. Imagine: the Bible, a cure for illiteracy!

We have come a long way since using the Bible as a textbook to teach reading and writing. Not only do the poor have options for education on days other than Sunday, but we have learned so much about how people learn. Is your Sunday School attendance dropping off? School teachers have changed the way they teach. Perhaps the traditional way of doing Sunday School no longer works in your setting. You want what you teach to "stick." You want children to enjoy coming to Sunday School and to keep coming back. You want to have children hear the life-saving message of the Gospel. Maybe it's time to give Workshop Rotation a try.

In a nutshell, Workshop Rotation can be described as "VBS every week." Kids love VBS! It's noisy, colorful, active, and fun. Kids learn one core subject the whole week long. The subject matter is taught again and again through a variety of methods, and you know the kids have learned it because they sing the songs, cling to their projects, and wear their hand-painted T-shirt for weeks!

It's the same thing with Workshop Rotation. Last year, at Mount Olive in Anoka, MN, we taught five Workshop Rotation units that spread from the Sunday after Labor Day to the Sunday before Memorial Day. We taught children all about the Bible stories of Noah's ark, Mary and Joseph's journey to Bethlehem, Joseph and his amazing coat, what it means to be Easter People, and the apostle Paul. If these same stories were taught in a traditional Sunday School format, the lesson would take between five to ten weeks of the thirty-four week school year.

Instead, we taught each story as a unit for approximately four to six weeks. The children learned more about the story than they ever had before. Even the Rotation Teachers and Shepherds learned things they never knew! Repetition is at the heart of learning, and when our beloved Bible stories are told again and again in new, fun, and exciting ways, children are more likely to remember them. They may even be encouraged to bring their friends!

Large-Group Time

As our team first prepared to make the transition from traditional Sunday School to Workshop Rotation, we talked to other people who had broken the transition ground before us. We heard about their frustrations and blessings, their wishes and successes. One of the things we heard loud and clear was that what was needed was some sort of a transition piece to bridge unit to unit. In other words, we needed to help children see how the story of Joseph is related to the story of Christmas, how the story of Christmas is related to the story of Easter, and how the story of Easter is related to the story of the apostle Paul. Our solution to that problem was to schedule a *Seed Planting* and a *Harvest* transition week for every unit.

Seed Planting

The first week of our rotation unit is called *Seed Planting*. We call it that because when we gather all the children, the Shepherds, the Rotation Teachers, and parents, our aim is to sow the seeds—to cast the vision for the rotation unit to come in the next four to six weeks. This Seed Planting lasts the entire hour and is held in our chapel. During this time, we tell the story of the unit we are embarking upon through a means we have chosen (drama, puppets, a pantomime using the kids themselves, video, or whatever else fits). We select some sort of theme song for the unit, which the children sing every week at opening to help with continuity. If we have a drama, we have the same actor portray the main character throughout the entire unit. For one of our rotations, our Opening Leader had the children make and decorate journals on Seed Planting Sunday. The kids wrote and drew pictures in their journals every week of this unit telling what they learned that day.

Lessons Learned

Only students in grades 1–4 participate in our Workshop Rotation. Our preschool students benefit from the stability of a self-contained classroom. We felt that older students might consider the rotations too "childish" and thus be tempted toward disruption. The decision of what grades to involve in workshops should be tailored to your particular situation.

Weekly Openings

During the rotation weeks, we have a 15-minute opening led by our Opening Leader. We are blessed to have our old sanctuary to use as our chapel. All students in first through fourth grade meet in the chapel at our designated start time. Parents feel more comfortable having a central location at which to drop off their children each week. During the 15-minute opening, the Opening Leader leads the singing of the theme song, has additional dramas or puppets to tell more details about the story, takes an offering, celebrates baptismal birthdays, and generally casts the vision of the current unit. It's amazing how quickly that time goes by, especially if parents are in the habit of dropping their children off late. One of the most difficult parts about Opening is starting on time, even when there are only a few children.

Harvest Time

Once the rotations are completed (more detail on these later), there is a one-hour slot scheduled in our chapel. This time, there is a wrap-up of the just completed unit, along with a bridging event or discussion that ties this unit to the upcoming one. The rest of the time is spent on the Seed Planting for the next unit.

End of the Year Celebration

At Mount Olive, our Sunday School program is called Kids for Christ. On the last day of our Kids for Christ classes, we held a Harvest Time Celebration Event. We enticed parents to join us by promising coffee and donuts as well as original performances by their children showcasing what they had learned over the past nine months. Each of our four classes was assigned the task of picking their favorite rotation unit and in a few minutes—in their own way—demonstrating what they had learned in that unit. We built an extra week into the calendar just before the celebration as a rehearsal time for the group's Shepherds to meet with them and encourage their creative juices.

This Harvest Time Celebration turned out even better than I had hoped. Because it was by the children and for the children, their performances were original and inspiring. The fourth graders put together a fifteen-question quiz on facts about the story of Noah's ark. They quizzed the children and their parents with multiple-choice questions on things like which kind of birds Noah released from the ark and in what order.

The first and third graders joined forces and did a freeze-frame performance of each of the five units. At rehearsals, the Shepherds helped the children get into position as various characters of the stories, like Noah, Mrs. Noah, and the animals of their choice two by two. Then the Shepherds told them to freeze and took a picture. The pictures were then loaded onto a laptop, which was available for the children to look at the following week for their performance time. In this way, the children were easily, and surprisingly quickly, able to see where to stand.

The second graders chose the apostle Paul unit as their favorite. They made two posters. One told about Saul and how he was persecuting Christians and the other about Paul and how he was transformed and began helping Christians. Then the second graders performed a made-up chant about how Paul was transformed to the beat of "We Will Rock You." I was nearly in tears as I saw the four grades of children having fun with Bible stories in ways that they themselves engineered.

Classroom Environment

Another thing that makes Workshop Rotation unique is that the kids rotate from classroom to classroom each week. We have six rooms dedicated as Kids for Christ classrooms. There are several rotations that are the children's favorites, so we make sure to have those available every time. That means that one of the classrooms is a dedicated science rotation room, one is the cooking rotation room, and one is our art rotation room. The other three classrooms vary depending on our needs.

In each rotation classroom, there is a different group of kids learning about the current unit through a different learning style in a different environment. Since the children rotate rooms, they don't really have a classroom of their own. This has both pros and cons. One positive is that we can utilize more of the Body of Christ by recruiting "Environment People" to decorate the six classrooms. These are people who do not wish to serve on Sunday mornings for whatever reason but still have a passion for helping children learn Bible stories. They also have a talent for art and decorating. We have asked these people to adopt one or two rooms for the school year, decorating those rooms according to the unit theme.

Laura, a member of our Environment Team, was in charge of our science rotation room for the past school year. She painted a giant road on poster board for our unit on the journey to Bethlehem and hung it on the wall. Then she painted posters of Mary and Joseph on their donkey along the road. The kids loved the colorful wall hangings in their classroom, which enhanced their learning visually.

For the next unit, Laura took down Mary and Joseph and put up Jacob and his son Joseph along the same road. This time, however, there were sheep grazing nearby, and Joseph's coat was a very colorful piece of wallpaper fabric. This clever volunteer then took down Jacob and Joseph and put Saul on that same road in the scene where he was being blinded by God's light! Talk about working smarter, not harder!

Staff

Recruit a Great Team

Don't try to run a Workshop Rotation Sunday School all by yourself. A team makes all the difference in the world. The real beauty of Workshop Rotation is that you recruit your staff (by *staff* I mean unpaid staff, i.e., volunteers) based on their gifts, abilities, interests, and time schedule.

If you know someone who loves science, invite that person to be a science rotation teacher. Tell him or her that instead of teaching for nine months, he or she will be teaching one lesson four times (or however many groups of children you have) to different ages of kids for one unit (or more if he or she chooses). If you have someone who wants to help with children's ministry but doesn't have a lot of time, ask that person to be a Shepherd for the year. Explain that there is no lesson preparation required for Shepherds. Their sole job is to develop relationships with kids as they guide them from rotation to rotation. An ideal staffing for Workshop Rotation might look like this:

- Core Team—includes Leader, an Administrative Assistant, a Supplies Coordinator, a Shepherd Coach, and an Opening Leader.
  - ☆ Leader—champions the entire program, including leading the Core Team.
  - ☆ Administrative Assistant—handles the paperwork and communication among the team members.
  - ☆ Supplies Coordinator—works to procure supplies required in all areas.
  - ☆ Shepherd Coach—trains and equips the groups' Shepherds.

- ☆ Opening Leader—leads the large-group openings each week.
- Prayer Team—people who faithfully pray for the staff, the children, and children who have yet to be invited to Sunday School.
- Rotation Teachers—responsible for one lesson per rotation per unit.
- Shepherds—two for each group of children, for the entire year.
- Environment People—number required depends on how many rooms each person is willing to decorate.
- Marketing/Communications—take pictures, write articles for church newsletter, create and put up posters to communicate the schedule.

Difference between Shepherds and Rotation Teachers

It's very important to have a clear distinction between the Shepherds and the Rotation Teachers when you recruit staff. I recommend putting together a Ministry Position Description for each so there are no surprises.

Shepherds are the people who commit to being with the same group of kids for the entire season. This would be similar to a traditional Sunday School teacher, except the Shepherd is not responsible for teaching, only for nurturing the children, building relationships with them and their parents, and making connections with the children when they miss class. The Shepherds also pray with and for the children and, if necessary, handle discipline issues while the Rotation

Lessons Learned

Sometimes, when we recruit volunteers for Sunday School we ask them to take on roles outside of their skill or comfort level. By utilizing volunteers with specific skills, it makes recruiting easier. For example, our Environment People love decorating and being crafty, but aren't responsible for being a teacher for an entire year. Likewise, since teachers aren't responsible for decorating their room with each change of unit, they can spend more time on their teaching preparations. It's a good thing for everyone.

Teachers are teaching.
They may also do some summarizing once the lesson is complete for the morning. They stay with the children at all times and are the first there and the last to leave. In terms of attitude, they should also be prepared to jump in and play with the kids. When the kids are singing, they should sing loud and clear, setting an example of desired behavior.

Rotation teachers are responsible for preparing and teaching the actual rotation lesson. They prepare a lesson that they then teach several times, depending on how many groups or grades you have. Rotation Teachers need to consider the age of the children in their audience each week. In other words, a Rotation Teacher could expect a fourth grader to journal several things in a short period of time, but to ask a first grader to do so is an exercise in frustration for both child and teacher.

Rotation Teachers should not have to discipline or quiet the children. The Shepherds are in the classroom with the children and should deal with behavior issues during the rotation lesson. Ideally, there will be at least three adults per classroom: two Shepherds and one Rotation Teacher. In the event that a Shepherd is ill or unable to attend, there is always that second Shepherd in attendance, which means there is still a safe adult-child ratio from a risk-management perspective. In a recent Kids for Christ season, there were only two weekends where one of our classes had no teacher. Every other week, the Shepherds recruited their own subs from the pool of parents. It's easy to grab a parent as a Shepherd substitute when you go with Workshop Rotation as there is no preparation involved, only the desire to ensure the safety of a group of children while showing them the love of Jesus.

Opening Leader

The Opening Leader should be someone who can capture the attention of a large group of children as well as adults. They should be bold, animated, and willing to be silly on occasion. They also need to be able to keep to a tight schedule, since Openings can only be 15 minutes long or the Rotation Teachers will be shorted time from the "meat" of the unit, the rotation lesson. This Opening Leader doesn't have to *do* everything, but they must be able to organize the Seed Plantings, Harvest Times, and Openings; recruit drama people; and administrate the events.

Things to Consider

Change the Name

When something major happens to someone in the Bible, a name change often accompanies that event, for example, Abram to Abraham, Jacob to Israel, and Saul to Paul. When our congregation made the decision to change from a traditional Sunday School model to Workshop Rotation, we changed the name from Sunday School to Kids for Christ to help communicate that change.

Our congregation is blessed to have many talented artists. One of them, Joy, is a wiz with graphic design. She created a wonderful logo for us that we used to make posters announcing this exciting change. We paired that logo and the new name Kids for Christ with such words as "fun, exciting, colorful, active, and new" in our marketing to help create a positive buzz around the event.

Supplies

We love plastic bins! Rotation teachers each have a large bin that they pick up in the Kids for Christ office each week that holds their supplies. The Shepherds also have plastic bins that hold whatever supplies they need for the week as well as a number of items they use regularly, like markers, nametags, and pencils. Different Shepherds have different needs/desires and so some keep additional items in their bins like snacks or stickers.

We always have the usual supplies on hand (markers, paper, pipe cleaners, glitter, chalk, etc). However, since the Workshop Rotation model is a more supply-heavy program than traditional Sunday School, Chris, our supplies coordinator, does an excellent job of making sure that everyone on the team has what they need, when they need it. She created a supplies request form to e-mail our staff. She then goes shopping for their supplies and makes sure they are put in the correct bins. This is so very beneficial, especially when it comes to reimbursement. If one person buys all the supplies, there is only one person to reimburse—only one person to whom you need to teach your reimbursement procedure. For example, when Tracy, our Art Rotation Leader, needed sixty nativity craft stick sets ordered, Chris took care of it and Tracy could concentrate on the lesson preparations.

Openings vs. Closings

Perhaps your church would do well with having the children gather together at the end of the hour instead of the beginning. You could have a closing time instead of an opening time. Our staff considered this because of the number of students who were missing the opening due to late arrival. We opted to stick with openings, however, as we deduced that chronically late children (read: chronically late parents) would then be late to the rotation classroom and perhaps miss the meat of the lesson. You'll have to decide what is best for your church.

Rotate Classrooms or Rotate Teachers?

Even though we had handed out a schedule to parents at the beginning of each unit, and even though we had our schedule posted in about ten different locations around church as well as on our Web site, a couple of people still complained about not knowing where to pick up their kids each week since they were in one of six rotation rooms.

This coming year we are considering having the Rotation Teachers rotate rooms instead of the children rotating rooms. The benefit of this is parents will have a consistent place to pick up their children. However, there are several downsides to this plan. There will naturally be less variety to the program since kids will be staying in the same room. Rotation Teachers won't be able to have things set up in the same room for the duration of the unit, and the Shepherds will be responsible for decorating their own classrooms. It will be interesting to see after this next year which way works best for our church.

Snacks

Our transition to Workshop Rotation was overwhelmingly positive. There was really only one complaint in addition to the minor issue mentioned above. A member of our Core Team mentioned that the children would probably complain if they didn't get a snack every week in class as they had in traditional Sunday School. Right now, the kids only get a snack in the Cooking Rotation. With food allergies a major concern, not having snacks became a relief rather than a burden.

Calendar

If possible, decide your entire year's rotation units before you begin recruiting staff. This way, your Rotation Teachers will be able to say yes or no based on not only their topical interests (whatever units you have chosen to do this year), but also their personal calendars. As you choose units, try to imagine the connection between the units. For example, it's pretty easy to see the connection between the Christmas story and the Easter story. However, it can be harder to bridge the story of the tower of Babel and a lesson on stewardship. Once you have a year-at-a-glance calendar completed, you can then take a look at the individual units and plan the types of rotations you will use. You will also then be able to plan and recruit for your Seed Plantings and Harvest Times dates. For a sample year-at-a-glance calendar see page 52.

Once you have your year-at-a-glance calendar completed, you can make a calendar for each unit. I recommend making lots of copies of this calendar. Put them up as posters in numerous places so parents can easily locate their child's current rotation. Also, hand out a copy to each Rotation Teacher, each Shepherd, and every family. See the sample rotation schedule on page 53.

Rotation Planning

As you consider how to decide what rotations to develop, let's consider the story of Noah. You are probably familiar with the story of Noah's ark. Maybe you've even heard it a hundred times. In a nutshell, the story goes like this:

People were bad. Very bad. God chose Noah to build an ark. Noah obeyed God and built the ark. God sent all the animals to the ark two by two. God sent rain for forty days and nights. The world flooded and everyone died. Noah and his family stayed in the ark for a long time until the ark landed on a mountain. Noah sent birds out to see if he and his family could come out of the ark. When they finally came out, God sent a rainbow as a promise that He would never again destroy the entire world with a flood.

This Old Testament account is a favorite story for many people, children and adults alike. How can you teach this story *again* and not bore people? With Workshop Rotation, children (and adults) will learn this story through multiple learning styles and multiple learning environments. They won't get bored because they will be using all five senses, moving around, touching things, smelling things, and applying what they have learned. Doing so, they will be more and more likely to retain the information, not to mention they'll be having more fun.

> **Lessons Learned**
>
> For more information on brain development and why Workshop Rotation works for children, try doing a Web search on "Gardner's multiple intelligences."

People learn by combining visual (seeing), auditory (hearing), and kinesthetic (touching or actively doing) input. For our purposes, we want to know how children can see, hear, and touch the story of Noah's ark to more thoroughly learn and retain it.

Nina, our Science Rotation Teacher, took the children outside our church building and paced off the size of the ark. They walked from one end of the church parking lot to the other, and found out that Noah's ark was larger than our church building and parking lot! Physically walking the distance from the imaginary stem to stern of the ark gave the kids a better idea how God could put elephants, lions, bears, alligators, kangaroos, bats, mosquitoes, and butterflies in one floating zoo. By actively pacing off the size of the ark, the children got involved in the lesson kinesthetically and visually. I watched the kids come in from the parking lot that Sunday morning, they were wide eyed and energized, and the Shepherds were coming into the building saying things like "I had no idea it was *that* big!"

In one 45-minute lesson, the kids had an increased appreciation for the magnitude of the task Noah had in building this huge ark, caring for the animals, and how Noah built the ark to God's specifications. The story can then be "brought home" by helping the children see how as Noah by faith obeyed God even though the task was huge, we also live daily by faith in Christ.

The next week, after their 15-minute Opening, this same group of kids will rotate to a different classroom to learn even more about the story of Noah's ark through a 45-minute Music Rotation. They will sing a favorite song about Noah (who doesn't still love to sing "Rise and Shine"?) and make rain sticks out of rice and paper towel rolls while they learn about how Noah worshiped God and how we worship God too.

The next week, this same group of kids will learn more about Noah through a different rotation. Maybe it's a Cooking Rotation (half of a pita shaped kind of like an ark and the different foods animals ate) or an Art Rotation (finger-painting a rainbow on butcher paper on the Art Rotation room wall while learning about the covenant God made with Noah and how that promise stands today). The possibilities are endless.

You can tailor your rotations based on the curriculum as well as the gifts, talents, and interests of your congregation. In other words, if you know a person who is good with technology, why not invite her to teach the story of Noah's ark through computers via PowerPoint or Flash? Or if you know a person who has a passion for drama or storytelling, invite him to come and teach a unit with his skills. The cool part about it is that they'll teach one lesson several times to each age group and then have the option of taking the next unit off. There is significantly less burnout with Workshop Rotation because people have the option to say yes to some opportunities and no to others. Some other rotation ideas are computer, music, storytelling, puppetry, drama, video, and games. The list is only as limited as your imagination.

Conclusion

Workshop Rotation provides a fabulous way to teach children beloved Bible stories through repetition, different learning styles, and an exciting environment. Workshop Rotation allows you to explore new ways to recruit your Sunday School staff. People are invited to serve according to their interests, gifts, and as their schedule permits.

Year-at-a-Glance Chart

Date	Unit	Notes
9.9.07	Rally Day	Everyone meets in main sanctuary
9.16.07	Seed Planting: Noah's ark	1 hour in chapel with grades 1–4
9.23.07–10.21.07	5 Noah rotations: Art, Music, Games, Cooking, Science	Opening for grades 1–4 in Chapel.
10.28.07	Special! Missions: Matt & Angie and family guest speakers.	Together in Chapel for the whole hour. Encourage parents to attend.
11.4.07	Harvest Time: Noah, missions. Seed Planting: Journey to Bethlehem	1 hour in chapel with grades 1–4.
11.11.07–12.16.07	6 Journey to Bethlehem Rotations: Science, Creative Cookery, Games, Music movement, Storytelling, Art	Opening for grades 1–4 in Chapel.
12.23.07–12.30.07	No Kids for Christ	No Kids for Christ
1.6.08	Harvest Time: Journey to Bethlehem/Seed planting: Joseph	1 hour in chapel with grades 1–4.
1.13.08–1.27.08	Joseph rotation	Opening for grades 1–4 in Chapel.
2.3.08	Harvest Time: Joseph/Seed Planting: Easter	1 hour in Chapel with grades 1–4.
2.10.08–3.16.08	Easter Rotation	Opening for grades 1–4 in Chapel.
3.23.08	No Kids for Christ	No Kids for Christ
3.30.08	Harvest Time: Easter/Seed Planting: Paul	1 hour in Chapel with grades 1–4.
4.6.08–5.4.08	Paul Rotation	Opening for grades 1–4 in Chapel.
5.11.08	Shepherds meet in classrooms with children to prepare Harvest Time Celebration performance	Each grade will be assigned one of the rotation rooms in advance.
5.18.08	Harvest Time Celebration Sunday; Last day of Kids for Christ	In Chapel. Grades 1–4 will do a presentation they have created on their own for each other and their parents.
5.25.08	Memorial Day	No Kids for Christ

Joseph Rotation Schedule

(Please pick up your 1st–4th grader promptly by 10:15 a.m.)

Opening begins at 9:15 a.m. in the Chapel (Old Sanctuary).

Parents will pick up their children promptly at 10:15 a.m. according to the following schedule.

Grade	Shepherds	1.6.08	1.13.08	1.20.08	11.27.08	2.3.08	2.10.08
1st	Terri J. & Jacki B.	Begin Joseph Rotation: All 1st–4th graders will meet in Chapel for the entire hour.	Science (Room 121/3)	Music (Room 1105)	Art (Room 1109)	Games (Room 1103)	Begin Easter Rotation: All 1st–4th graders will meet in Chapel for the entire hour.
2nd	Lori M. & Melissa G.		Games (Room 1103)	Science (Room 121/3)	Music (Room 1105)	Art (Room 1109)	
3rd	Jane S. & Angie S.		Art (Room 1109)	Games (Room 1103)	Science (Room 121/3)	Music (Room 1105)	
4th	Jerry H.		Music (Room 1105)	Art (Room 1109)	Games (Room 1103)	Science (Room 121/3)	

7

Rotation and the Small Church

By Sandi Grupe

"Rotation Sunday School will not work in my church . . . it's too small!" What? Great opportunities await the small church with rotation Sunday School. You might just find that your small Sunday School begins to grow as your rotational model adds life and excitement to Sunday mornings.

"We share space and cannot theme our rooms."

One of the exciting aspects of rotation Sunday School for children is the themed and decorated rooms and spaces that are created. This adds energy to the classroom and creates anticipation among the children. Small churches might find this challenging as space is often shared with other ministries or the congregation itself is portable and cannot transform a classroom into a themed rotation space for kids. This is an issue, but don't lose heart. Sometimes not being able to theme a classroom for a specific type of rotation can work to your advantage. Do you have limited space? Create shorter rotations, maybe three weeks instead of four or five. Have six or more rotation ideas/themes and rotate through them during the year. Consider staying in one place each Sunday and having the rotation come to you. Children know which classroom is theirs and report to it each Sunday but still have the surprise of a new rotation/activity awaiting them. This eases the confusion that will arise trying to switch classrooms that cannot be predesignated for a particular theme. Do not underestimate the importance of decorations and themes to the energy of your program, even if your conditions are less than desirable. Do your best to create portable décor that identifies the rotation and generates excitement for the lesson.

"We do not have enough classroom space."

Think outside of the box with the use of your space! Smaller classes and a wider variety of rotation themes open the door to greater possibilities. Go outside for a messy science experiment rotation, a journey through the wilderness with the Israelites, or a prayer walk! Consider the impact of a rotation in the narthex/foyer as you talk about making disciples and reaching out to those God brings into our midst. Use the sanctuary for rotations on worship, the Sacraments, music, and more.

"We do not have enough kids for a traditional four-to-six-week rotation."

Turn it into a three-week rotation and combine age groups as developmentally appropriate. If you only have enough kids to give you sufficient critical mass for two rotations, then spend the first two Sundays in rotations and combine the two groups on the third Sunday for a joint rotation. This can work well if you keep in mind the developmental differences within your age groups. For example, spend the third week in the "cinema" for a movie rotation. Create discussion questions that vary in complexity and break down into two groups for discussion. Create a life-size board game as a combined activity and have two sets of questions for your two groups.

"Rotation Sunday School is too labor intensive and we do not have enough volunteers."

It doesn't have to be. Use some willing volunteers from the congregation for three-week commitments or the length of your rotation. Three weeks is not a long commitment, so try pulling in some individuals and groups that do not traditionally volunteer in children's ministry. Consider designing specific rotations for these groups that utilize their interests and strengths. This is a great opportunity for intergenerational ministry. The benefits of this will spread far beyond your Sunday morning classroom. Some rotations are not as labor intensive and do not need outside crews to be brought in. In this case, use your classroom Shepherds as the lead for the rotation if the size of your classroom allows it.

"It is impossible to find a rotation curriculum that is written with the small church in mind."

Yes, it is difficult with any Sunday School model to find the "perfect" curriculum. Rotation Sunday School curriculum is most often written with a large church mindset. Be prepared to invest some time and creativity in reviewing the curriculum and rewriting it as necessary to fit your congregation's personality, style, and space. There are many wonderful resources on the Web that can be used for support and inspiration as you set your mind to this task.

8

Adapting Curriculum

By Christine Eid

Introduction

In spring of 2005, the Board of Education at my church decided it needed to do something to revitalize Sunday School. Attendance was decreasing, and there was little enthusiasm from students. It was becoming difficult to find adults who were willing to commit to a year of teaching. What's more, by February they were tired and their weariness showed in the classrooms. We knew we needed to look for some way to make kids excited about hearing the special message of Jesus, our Savior.

During the summer, a group of committed parents came together to brainstorm and discuss what our options were. The initial talk was about painting the classrooms to make them more inviting while also incorporating some special events into the scheduled curriculum. But one parent expressed the concern that we could change the classrooms all we wanted, but if we didn't change some of the format as well, the attitude wouldn't change. Then someone shared their experience with site-rotation Sunday School, and the energy level increased immediately. On August 1, the decision was made to make the switch. Sunday School would start in a month. Could it happen? With enthusiasm and growing excitement, many volunteers put in countless hours to make it happen.

Looking back now, one year later, we can say it was a success. Children got excited and attendance increased, with new families joining us throughout the year. New people participated in teaching throughout the year as well, and there was never the weariness of years past. As soon as the year was over, people started meeting to plan the "next stage" of the program and what needed to be done over the summer months.

While not for everyone, site-rotation Sunday School breathed new life into a program that was struggling in our church community. As we continue to grow and develop, we see how this model continues to meet the needs of children and adults as they grow in their faith and share the Gospel with others. Can site rotation work for you? The ideas in this resource are flexible and can work with your specific situation with very little modification. It is our hope that this guide will assist you as you consider adopting site rotation in your children's ministries.

Part 1: What Is Site-Rotation Sunday School?

Site-rotation Sunday School is a flexible option of coordinating classes into different settings and groups during the Sunday School time. Concordia Publishing House's Growing in Christ curriculum lends itself to this adaptation, as the scope and sequence are the same for all ages. Activities from each grade level can be adapted and incorporated into the lesson outlines for each site in the rotation. It works well with our new format.

There are many benefits to the site-rotation format. First and foremost is the flexibility it gives your teaching staff. One of the biggest difficulties with Sunday School identified by churches is finding teachers to commit for an entire year. The site-rotation model allows for individuals to work in areas that they are specifically gifted in and for shorter periods of time. So, instead of finding all-around classroom teachers, you can draw on people's strengths. It's easier to recruit someone to teach just music or to handle only arts and crafts. Plus, leaders may be recruited for one week, a month, or a quarter, depending on the format that is selected for the site rotations.

A second benefit is that the rotation model allows students different activities in different settings. In today's world, where children are accustomed to a variety of media and stimuli around them, the rotation model reaches children in different ways, adapting lessons to accommodate different learning styles while allowing greater opportunities for creativity throughout the education hour.

A third benefit is that while individuals can teach children in areas that they are particularly gifted in, relationships actually seem stronger in site rotation. Volunteer guides are used whose sole role is to "shepherd" and get to know children. (Definitions of all volunteers and roles will follow later.)

Finally, site rotation also lends itself to using the gifts of others who might not be gifted teachers but excel in the areas of administration, decorating, missions, and so on. Adapting the overall program allows more people to be involved in ways that meet their passions for spreading the Gospel of Jesus Christ to others.

Part 2: Options of Site-Rotation Sunday School

There are different options for the format of the site-rotation Sunday School. There are benefits to each option, but choose the ones that are best for your program's goals and space.

Opening: All these options begin with a large-group Opening. The Director Guide for Growing in Christ each quarter is an excellent resource for the opening portion of the education hour. An overall outline is included as well as suggestions for preparing your worship space. A short devotional talk is included in this resource as well. (Think about incorporating elements of worship too. This will help the children understand the worship structure of the congregation.) Smaller Sunday Schools may choose to have the opening with all students together. Older students can be assigned to younger children as mentors to assist in the activities and seating. An advantage of having all the students together is that this depicts the unity of the Body of Christ and exemplifies how corporate worship of the congregation happens. One disadvantage is that one huge gathering limits the range of music and the depth of presentations since material needs to be accessible to children of all ages.

Larger Sunday Schools should consider using two age-appropriate Openings. In this way, the music and message can be crafted to an age-appropriate audience. However you choose to do your Opening, attention should be given to developing an exciting opportunity for children to join together for praise and worship of their Lord and Savior. Allow students to be involved through the reading of Scripture, singing, and preparing the worship space. As students are involved, their excitement will be contagious, generating more enthusiasm.

After the Opening, different options are available for site rotations using the Growing in Christ curriculum. Each of these can be additionally modified to meet the needs of your Sunday School.

Option 1

God Speaks—Students remain in the large group for the "God Speaks" section of the lesson. A leader gifted in storytelling tells the Bible story (or uses other media such as video, books, drama, etc., to tell the story) to everyone and reviews the story with the group. (See later in this resource for suggestions on using the Teacher Guides in preparation for this section.)

Music—Students remain in the large group for a music session with a leader gifted in music to learn hymns and songs tied in with the lesson. Materials are provided in the curriculum to assist with this area.

We Live—Break up students into small groups by age/grade level for discussion of the lesson using the age-appropriate materials. This is an excellent opportunity for relationship building and for a greater in-depth discussion of the lesson. Leaders of the small groups must prepare for discussion questions but do not need to prepare an entire Bible story presentation.

Closing—Students return to the large group to join in a common Closing. The Bible story is briefly reviewed again. Close with music and prayers.

Option 2

Following the large-group opening, children are split into groups, each led by a Shepherd (a guide that sticks with the group each week). The groups rotate every 10–15 minutes to different sites as outlined below. Staff for each station will lead the activities with the Shepherds guiding the children from one activity to the next. The Shepherds provide comfort and consistency for the kids throughout the lesson and from week to week.

God Speaks—The leader uses the “God Speaks” section from the Teacher Guide to tell the Bible story.

Music—The leader uses CDs and other musical materials to teach a song relating to the story theme.

We Live—A leader assists the Shepherds in discussing the application portion of the Teacher Guide.

Arts and Crafts—Using the student items and Teacher Guide reproducible pages, the leader assists students in making a take-home piece to reinforce the lesson of the day.

Snack—This leader prepares and serves a simple snack and beverage, possibly tied in with the lesson for the day.

Games—The Growing in Christ curriculum has many suggestions of review games for each week’s story. (A separate workshop may be utilized to use these resources.)

Closing—This can be done either at each group’s final site or as a large group using a closing activity found in the Teacher Guide.

Option 3 (A combination of options 1 and 2)

God Speaks—As with option 1, keep students together for the telling of the Bible story in a large-group setting.

We Live—Students move into small groups for a short discussion of the story using questions suggested in this section of the Teacher Guide.

Stations—In a large area, have tables of the different stations described in option 2. Students can move around to the stations as they desire, focusing on activities that fit their learning style and interests. Additional stations that might be set up include a Drama area for students to re-enact the Bible story, a Service area incorporating a service project for the month or quarter, and a Reading area with Bible story books for students who wish to read more about the story on their own.

Option 4:

In this option, one story is selected to be the focus of a four-week period of classes. Workshops are then planned with a variety of presentations of the story of the month, utilizing an in-depth activity to reinforce the story. In this model, different workshops may use the varying forms of Bible story presentation found in the different Teacher Guides, as well as more of the reinforcement activities. While children will learn fewer Bible stories over the course of the year with this option, students who miss a Sunday will still learn the story. Those who are in attendance on a more regular basis receive a weekly reinforcement of the story.

As with the other options, a large-group Opening introduces the topic of the week/month and works on a musical piece. An advantage of this option is that more time can be allowed for the Opening because the other workshops have more time to do their activities as well. Following the large-group Opening, students and their Shepherds will go to one workshop for the remainder of the time that Sunday. These workshops might include the following (although more are possible):

Music—As described in the other options, the leader uses the Growing in Christ CDs and other musical materials to teach one or two songs that focus on the theme of the month. If you use this option, consider having the students sing the song they learn in worship at the end of the month as a way to highlight the children's ministry of your congregation.

Drama—The story is reinforced as the students act out the story in different forms.

Arts and Crafts—After hearing the story in a new form, students complete a more in-depth craft to take home and have as a daily reminder of the month's story.

Cooking—The leader presents the story followed by a cooking activity. Students eat while reviewing the lesson.

Video—Students watch a video relating to the story of the month. Discussion follows the video to review key points of the story.

Service/Missions—If your Sunday School has a regular mission project or is participating in one through the missions department, this workshop can be an opportunity to explain further what is happening in the project. It also provides an opportunity for hands-on experiences tied in with the mission project. Consider a service project as an opportunity for students to reach out to individuals within your community or congregation.

Memory Work—This might be incorporated into other workshops or be a workshop on its own. In this area, the focus is on learning the Bible memory verse (and possibly catechism passages) tied in with the lesson. Growing in Christ provides several resources to assist you with this workshop.

At the end, students may remain in their workshops as those leaders host closing activities using materials from the Teacher Guides or there can be a large-group Closing where students can join together in music and prayer before being sent out as witnesses in the world.

Part 3: Definitions and Job Descriptions

The following terms and job descriptions further explain the site-rotation model. They will also assist you in recruiting volunteers. Use them to explain to individuals how the format works.

Workshops—These are centers focusing on a specific task or theme relating to the Bible story. Workshops may include, but are not limited to, arts and crafts, drama, music, storytelling, and so on.

General Job Descriptions—As recruitment begins for site-rotation Sunday School, it is important to prayerfully consider individuals who

- have the interest, skills, and ability to share the Gospel of Jesus Christ with children and their families;
- have a commitment to Christian education and outreach;
- enjoy working with children; and
- can donate the time. (For each area recruited, the time frame may vary. While individuals may commit to the entire program year, an advantage of site-rotation Sunday School is that it lends itself to smaller time commitments. Suggested time commitments for all staff other than Shepherds might be one month or one quarter. So that there is continuity for students throughout the year, it is ideal to have Shepherds commit for the entire program year.)

Opening and Closing Leaders—Plan and lead the Sunday School Opening (and Closing if there is one) so that students can grow in their knowledge of Jesus' love and God's grace. They

- are skilled in leading worship, singing, or making presentations;

- plan, set up, and lead Openings and Closings for time of commitment (one month or one quarter); and
- recruit helpers to assist, as needed. (These may include but are not limited to musicians, actors, puppeteers, and so on.)

Shepherds—Youth or adults who lead or "shepherd" a small group to different workshops. These individuals should make a longer commitment (think: a month, a quarter, or the entire education year).

Workshop Leaders—Youth or adults who lead a specific workshop for a designated period of time, as determined by your Sunday School program. See individual workshop titles for specific job descriptions.

Music—Teach songs and lead singing in Openings, Closings, and workshops.

- Use music to reinforce the Bible lessons and themes.
- Select and teach specific hymns and songs.
- Whenever possible, teach correlation between music and the Bible story and theme.
- Choose musical accompaniment options, using CDs found in the curriculum or live instruments.
- Recruit, coordinate, and practice with musicians as needed.
- Coordinate music and lead singing when there is a presentation in worship services or other opportunities.

Drama—Lead workshop focusing on the use of drama and/or puppets for the sharing of the Bible lesson and theme.

- Plan drama experiences utilizing students whenever possible.
- Prepare the drama settings, costumes, and props.
- Recruit helpers and actors as needed (although whenever possible use students in the drama process).
- Facilitate discussion after drama presentation to reinforce lesson points.

Arts and Crafts—Lead workshop focusing on the arts and crafts to reinforce the Bible story and theme. (This leader should be creative, artistic, and eager to share their faith with students during craft time.)

- Prepare a craft lesson tied in with the Bible story and theme.

- Purchase materials or arrange for donations of needed supplies.
- If using option 4, plan Bible story presentation as directed by the Sunday School Coordinator.
- Facilitate discussion after craft is completed to reinforce lesson points.

Cooking—Lead workshop using food to develop and reinforce the Bible lesson and theme.

- Plan theme-related snack based on the Bible story.
- Coordinate donations and food purchases.
- Check all registration forms for any food allergies, making adjustments as necessary.
- If using option 4, plan Bible story presentation as directed by the Sunday School Coordinator.
- Facilitate discussion after cooking activity to reinforce lesson points.

Video—Lead workshop using media to develop and reinforce the Bible lesson and theme.

- Select a theme-related video based on the Bible story (with the assistance of the Sunday School Coordinator).
- Purchase video, if necessary.
- Review video in preparation for showing.
- Coordinate popcorn and beverage for video showing, if desired for a movie theatre atmosphere.
- Confirm proper AV equipment is available for video showing.
- Introduce video to students; show video.
- Facilitate discussion after video to reinforce lesson points.

Service and Missions—Lead workshop that actively involves children and families in a mission project.

- With Sunday School Coordinator, select a mission or service project for current month or quarter from the Growing in Christ Web site (sundayschool.cph.org/missions).
- Plan activities to involve children and families in the mission or service project.
- Assist in publicizing the current Sunday School mission or service project in various publications, displays, and presentations.

- Educate students, parents, and congregation about the needs and opportunities of the project.
- Coordinate purchase of supplemental resources as needed.
- If using option 4, plan Bible story presentation as directed by the Sunday School Coordinator.
- Facilitate discussion after the activity to reinforce lesson points.
- Collect and distribute gifts for the mission project.

Memory Work—Lead workshop focusing on Bible memory verses related to the Bible story and theme.

- Plan verse- and theme-related activities based on the Bible story as provided in Growing in Christ.
- Recruit and coordinate volunteers, as needed, to assist.
- If using option 4, plan Bible story presentation as directed by the Sunday School Coordinator.
- Facilitate discussion after activity to reinforce lesson points.
- Use resources found in Growing in Christ.
- Bible Verse Songs (on Teacher CDs)
- Bible Words Puzzles (in Upper Grades and Jr. High Teacher Tools)

Part 4: Room and Space Setup

An advantage of the site-rotation model is that the setting, staging, and space are up to you. Some sites or workshops may be more elaborate than others, but all the ideas are flexible and can be adapted to fit your space and needs. General ideas for preparing your large-group Opening worship space can be found in the Director Guide. This checklist gives specifics for items needed and how to set up the space. As suggested, the more opportunities you provide for your children to interact with your environment and to be involved in a meaningful way with the worship experience, the more engaged the children will be.

One Large Room

If your education space is limited and you only have one large area for your children's education time, the site-rotation model can work well. In your space, have a section set for the large-group gathering. Chairs, pillows, or carpet squares may be used for this area, depending on how formal or informal you want things to be. When students break into small groups, they can move into designated areas within the room, sitting in circles. Chairs, pillows, carpet squares, or whatever seating pieces you use, can be moved with the children into their small-group times,and then brought back. If using options 2, 3, or 4, use tables for the designated activity areas, with students moving in a clockwise direction around the room during the breakout portion of the hour or month.

Multiple Rooms

If your education space includes multiple rooms, designate one room or space for your large-group Opening. Larger classes may be assigned to one room, which is then split into sub areas for discussion and activities. Furniture and decorations should fit the age group that is using that classroom. In option 2, 3, or 4, rooms may also be decorated to further develop the theme of the workshop. Some area decorating ideas:

God Speaks/Storytelling—Create a relaxed setting of pillows or carpet squares to sit on the floor. Use a small indoor/outdoor canopy tent with an area rug to set the space apart. Have bookshelves of Bible story books for students to look at if there is extra time throughout the morning hour.

Music—Decorate with musical instruments and notes on the wall. Have a variety of rhythm instruments and keyboards available for students to use if their musical interest is not vocal. An overhead projector or PowerPoint projector might be helpful, especially if you have a larger group together.

We Live—Cozy discussion areas help to facilitate discussion by creating a small-group atmosphere. Utilize pillows or carpet squares for a movable and adaptable space.

Arts and Crafts—The arts and crafts space should promote creativity. Have tables at appropriate heights for children and shelves for art materials. Decorations may include previous projects that children have worked on, pictures of Bible stories, or murals on the walls.

Snack/Cooking—Your cooking space should have a homey feel or reflect a café style. If it is possible, have a kitchen feel to the room, including café curtains, hot pads, aprons, and chef hats. Have large counters or tables for work space and smaller tables (if there is room) for the eating space.

Games—There are a variety of games in the Teacher Tools of Growing in Christ. Some are board games while others are active games that involve large motor skills. This should be a space with a lot of room, adaptable to the types of games utilized. For additional fun, consider making a life-size game board on the floor, using laminated construction paper squares, carpet squares, or a permanent design using different colored tiles.

Video—One of the most difficult aspects of using videos for larger groups is that not all children are able to see the TV monitor. If possible, project the movie on the wall or screen so all the children can easily see. Another option is to have tiered seating for students to look over each others' heads.

There are many options for room decorations and setup. They all depend on your budget and room availability. More examples of room decorations can be found at www.rotation.org. Do not be overwhelmed by these examples. Remember, a lot can be done with minimal expense—especially if you let your congregation know what your needs are for the program.

Part 5: Using and Adapting Growing in Christ

Because the Growing in Christ curriculum has a scope and sequence where all age levels have the same story each week, it is very conducive to using in a site-rotation format. While identifying different options for organizing site-rotations in part 2, some aspects of the curriculum were highlighted. Here are some additional ideas and ways to use and adapt Growing in Christ to meet your needs.

Openings—As noted previously, the Director Guide includes a suggested setup for your worship space, as well as an opening devotional talk that can be used each week. Some of the talks highlight aspects of a specific story, so be sure to review and confirm that it fits with the story that you are using that week. Additional resources and ideas are in each grade level's Teacher Guide. Share the resources with your volunteer(s) who leads Openings and Music. If you have more than one person doing this over the year, tear the books at the perforations and hand out the materials to the corresponding volunteers. CPH grants permission to make copies of select pages from the teacher manuals to give to volunteers in different roles. These are marked "Reproduced by permission." Depending on the format selected for your particular rotation model, the specifics of how to adapt the curriculum for the remainder of the education hour will vary. Following are suggestions for how to use the curriculum for each of the different rotation models.

Option 1:

God Speaks—With a large group of varying ages, the story presentation is a very important part of the morning's curriculum. Although the leader may be the same person who does the Opening, in order to allow for variety you should consider having someone different lead this section. Separate the Teacher Guide for the age groups according to the story and copy the "God Speaks" portion for the storyteller. The leader should review the options and select the presentation that best fits their style and excitement level, keeping in mind what has been used in previous weeks to allow for a variety of presentations. If puppets, drama, or video are being used to supplement the curriculum, make sure you've prepared by practicing ahead of time and having equipment ready and enough seating to allow the large group to be able to see the entire presentation clearly.

The "God Speaks" portion of the curriculum includes utilizing discussion with the student handouts. Have Shepherds use these as additional resources during the small-group discussion time. In this model, the large group should be presentation with some discussion, but save the worksheets for smaller gatherings.

Music—As with the Storytelling and Opening, the Music portion of the education time needs to be energetic, with a focus on using the gifts of children in music. If there are children who are not gifted in singing or who are uncomfortable singing, utilize them in other ways, including playing rhythm instruments, running PowerPoint screens with lyrics, or accompanying on piano, if they are gifted in this area. To provide a purpose to the Music time outside of learning new songs, plan to have children sing regularly in the large-group openings. Ask your pastor if the children may sing what they learn here in the worship service. This allows for visibility of the Sunday School to the rest of the congregation—and allows children to sing their praises to God in worship.

We Live—Provide Teacher Guides for the Shepherds to utilize during the discussion time. They should use the "We Live" section to spark discussion. This is also the time to use student leaflets and other resources from Growing in Christ. Besides discussing the story from the large-group presentation, Shepherds can also use the time as an opportunity for discussing how things are going for each of the students. Though there is a large-group Closing, use this time for a small-group prayer. Be sure to share prayer requests for the week.

Closing—To wrap up all the ideas, you might want the same person who led the Opening to lead your Closing, but another individual will work just as well. Copy the closing section of each of the Teacher Guides to give suggestions of the summary and review. The Bible Review Cards are an excellent resource to use as students come back to the large-group setting. Consider making a big game board with the questions and answers. After reviewing the story, use suggested activities for closing your time.

Option 2:

An additional staff member is needed for each activity station. Separate the Teacher Guides for each story, making copies for each of the station activities. Because station leaders will have all the age groups in their area, they can utilize aspects of each grade's guide in each presentation. Shepherds should be given the copies of their student handouts each week to be used at the appropriate stations. Staff for each station will lead the activities while Shepherds guide the children from one activity to the next (maintaining regular and comforting relationships).

Station specifics:

God Speaks—The leader uses the "God Speaks" section from the Teacher Guides to tell the Bible story. Because the curriculum identifies 20 minutes or more for this time, only a portion of each age groups' curriculum will be able to be used. Focus on telling the story, utilizing the suggested discussion questions as time allows.

Music—As noted in part 2, the leader may use CDs and other musical materials to teach a song relating to the story theme. Smaller groups allow one to focus each group on learning the words and their singing. Use this time to explain the background of the songs and what the meaning of phrases and words are. Growing in Christ provides a Teacher CD (levels Early Childhood–Upper Grades) with many songs and hymns that will work for your music rotation. The CDs also contain the sheet music for you to print and use.

We Live—The station leader facilitates the discussion as Shepherds assist students with handouts and activities. As with the "God Speaks" section, the curriculum usually suggests a longer period of time for this area. Identify key areas and focus on having an interactive discussion with students, keeping them actively involved. Use the Growing in Christ leaflets and other teacher tools.

Arts and Crafts—The Early Childhood and Lower Grade materials include craft pages in the student packets. These are easy to use in the time allotted for this station. In most cases, additional local resources will be needed to create crafts for Middle and Upper Grade levels. Several great resources are available from CPH at www.cph.org. Type "crafts" in the search box at the top of the page.

Snack—The Growing in Christ curriculum does not specifically identify snacks to incorporate into the lesson each week, so this is an area where a creative Snack Leader will come in handy. While a simple snack and beverage is all that is needed for this area, students enjoy having a snack that ties in with the lesson for the day (e.g., little fish crackers with the lesson where Jesus calls His disciples to be fishers of men). Be aware of student allergies while making plans for each week's snacks.

Games—Growing in Christ has many games for reviewing each week's story. Make copies of all the suggested options (review cards, reproducible games, etc.) for the station leader. Allow them to choose from the many options. Keep track of what games are used each week to ensure variety. Additional Bible games and puzzles can be found at www.cph.org or your local bookstore as your budget allows.

Closing—If this is done at each group's final site, make copies of the appropriate age-level closing from the Teacher Guides for each station leader. This may also be a role for the Shepherds. If so, make copies and give them to the Shepherds at the beginning of each month to allow them to review and prepare for their role in leading the closing discussion.

If you use the large-group Closing, consider having the Opening Leader also close the day (or task another volunteer). Make copies of all the closings in the curriculum, and allow the leader to pick and choose appropriate activities for the age groups. Encourage the leader to be energetic, sending the children on their way with one last review of the day's main points.

Option 3:

Because option 3 is a combination of options 1 and 2, refer to the curriculum adaptations previously noted for specifics. Suggestions for "God Speaks" and "We Live" can be found in option 1, while specifics on developing stations can be found under option 2. Since the "We Live" discussion is done separately, that station would be eliminated from the options student participate in. Option 3 may also be as structured or unstructured as the leadership is comfortable with. The stations may be in one large room (or smaller separate rooms) with children moving in a clockwise rotation to reach all the stations. Another option is to allow more freedom. With this method, students only attend the stations that they are specifically interested in. In this case, Shepherds act more like "floaters," watching that all of their students are actively involved and working in a specific area, but not directing them in an organized sequence.

If you go with the "freedom" option, be sure to also have a

quiet area for students to watch a video or read Bible story books as part of their overall station options. These areas are also helpful as time winds down, keeping students occupied if there is not enough time to start the activities at another station.

Option 4:

Growing in Christ is jam-packed with activities and options for your Sunday School. The Teacher Guides utilize a variety of activities so teachers can choose the activities that best fit their students and teaching style. This host of options means that some of the activities and materials will not be used on a weekly basis. Option 4 is a way to use more of the activities while focusing on fewer biblical accounts. In option 4, materials are used in a fuller capacity because one story is selected to be the focus of a four-week period. As noted previously, workshops are planned to provide a varied presentation of the story of the month. An in-depth activity is used to reinforce the story.

The administrator has a larger role in this model. He or she will select a general format of Bible story presentation for each workshop, being sure that different styles and mediums are used in each area. The administrator identifies the different presentation models noted in the different Teacher Guides while also identifying additional resources needed. He or she must then develop a packet from these resources with specifics of how to present the story in each setting. In some cases, each grade level's presentation may be easily adapted for other classes. In other cases, two distinct presentations may be necessary, one for younger students and another for older students.

In the monthly packet, include copies of the "Growing in the Word" resource from the Director and Teacher Guides for each volunteer. Encourage them to read through this commentary resource so they have the background for the story and know what is being focused on for the month.

The key to this method of site rotation is variety. If the same book or medium is used each week, students will become bored. However, if one week students hear the story read to them from Scripture or an age-appropriate Bible story book, the next week they see it in video form, and the next week they act it out using drama or puppets, the story is reinforced. Each form appeals to the different learning styles children have. Using the variety of presentation methods causes the story and concepts to be remembered better.

In this option, following the large-group Opening, students and their Shepherds go to one workshop for the remainder of the hour. Below are some of the basic workshops your program should consider, but the number and variety of your workshops is only limited by the gifts and imagination of your volunteers. (Although note that the number of workshops used each month should first be dependant on the number of classes your program has. Provide one workshop for each age group. If there are more age groups than weeks, students will not participate in all the workshops that month.)

Music—As described in the other options, the leader uses CDs and other musical materials to teach one or two songs focusing on the theme of the month. As noted with option 1, if there are children who are not gifted in singing or who are uncomfortable singing, utilize them in other ways, including playing rhythm instruments, running PowerPoint (for words on a large screen), or accompanying on piano—if they are gifted in this area. Again, a goal to keep in mind is to have the students sing the song they learn at the end of the month in worship. This not only highlights the children's ministry of your congregation, but directly involves the kids in the worship life of your church.

Drama—In this workshop, students have an opportunity to act out the story in different forms, reinforcing the story. Some grade levels may not have specific drama options highlighted, but the storytelling presentations in the Early Childhood and Lower Grade teacher manuals can be adapted for all ages. Creative leaders could also adapt their script right from the source, taking characters, dialogue, and narration right from the Bible.

The purpose of this chapter is to give general information, not specifics; however, here are some suggestions of how to adapt the curriculum for this workshop area: The Lower Grades Teacher Guide has many scripts easily adaptable to a variety of forms of drama and puppetry. If using storytelling figures, consider having kids make their own figures to tell the story at home. Each week, have students learn the story/drama to present to the upcoming class. Begin with the oldest age group, having them present the drama the following week to the next group. This second group then learns it for the following week. Youngest students will have the story presented to them and then work on their own presentation to tell parents at home.

Another option is for students to learn the story in drama form and then present the story during Sunday School openings. Students could also create their own books depicting the story. Consider having each class write the text for their book and identify scenes to act in still life. Using a digital camera, take pictures of the children acting out the scenes. Download the pictures to your computer and add them to the right pages of the text in your word processing or publishing program. (This idea provides a service opportunity for volunteers who are comfortable with computers but are not comfortable in direct contact with children [i.e., teaching]. During the week, they could put the books together so they are ready for distribution for the following week.)

Arts and Crafts—Because under this model students spend the entire time that week in this space, larger crafts and projects can be completed. First, tell the Bible story using one of the "God Speaks" presentations. Then introduce a more in-depth craft to reinforce the story and send home as a reminder. Consider using this workshop to involve students in a service project that incorporates art. Ideas include making quilt squares with the finished product sent to a family in need, special occasion greeting cards for congregational members, or, if you're really adventurous and space allows, have students create murals to decorate classrooms or hallways for now and the future. The Lesson Expanders at the end of each lesson in the Upper Grade Teacher Guide give additional suggestions for in-depth projects that can be adapted to all age levels.

Cooking—While specific ideas for cooking are not always included in Growing in Christ, students enjoy working with food and having the opportunity to eat afterwards. Be careful of food allergies while planning treats each month. Use the cooking time to discuss the lesson each week and review it again while eating the snack. Once again, this workshop lends itself to opportunities of service while students are having fun. Consider having students plan the treats for a fellowship time of the entire congregation. Then, work throughout the month to make enough to share. Another option is to make care packages for members away at college or in the military. (Be sure to have students make "thinking of you" cards to enclose in them.) Family members appreciate treats at home as well, and this is an excellent opportunity for students to share the story with other family members.

Video—Most Bible story videos average 30 minutes in length. This site-rotation format allows for a video to be shown with time for discussion following. To introduce the video, select one of the introductory activities found in the curriculum's Teacher Guides in the opening section. Many of these activities are excellent ways to set the stage for the story. After the introduction, show the video. Afterwards, discuss the video and review the key points of the story. Use one of the Teacher Guides for suggestions of what questions to ask. (This is an excellent opportunity to utilize the handouts in each student's pack.)

Games—As noted under option 2, the Growing in Christ curriculum has many review games for each week's story. Make copies of all the suggested options for the workshop leader for that story. Have materials from the teacher packets (review cards, reproducible games, etc.) available for the leader to use. Keep track of what games are used each month. Additional Bible game and puzzle resources can be found at www.cph.org or in your local bookstore.

If there is not a game workshop in a given month, consider having the review games available in a separate space. Shepherds can bring their groups to this space if they finish in their workshop early on a given week. Make available materials and easy instructions for all the students to use.

Additional suggestion: If you are using the game boards found in the teacher resources, consider laminating them before use to keep them in good condition.

Service/Missions—If your Sunday School has a regular mission project or is participating in one through the missions department, this workshop can be an opportunity to explain further what is happening in the project. It may also provide an opportunity for hands-on experiences tied in with the mission project. A service project might also be involved in this opportunity, allowing students to reach out to individuals within your community or congregation. Resources for mission projects are available through the Growing in Christ Mission Web site: sundayschool.cph.org/missions.

Memory Work—Learning God's Word through memorization is an important lesson we can share with our children. If you don't offer a specific memory work station, incorporate it into other workshops. The Director Guide CD has all of the Bible Memory words available for print while the CDs in the Teacher Packet have songs and rhythm resources. Pull the "Bible Words" portion of the curriculum from the Teacher Guides to generate additional ideas of how to help students memorize the weekly verse. Resources in the Teacher Tools for older students include reproducible Bible Words Puzzle Books. Utilize these puzzles as "time fillers" or create large-group activities to work through the puzzles together.

Closing

Because each workshop finishes at a different time, each workshop has its own (small-group) Closing. Use material from the Teacher Guides to develop these. Encourage Shepherds to talk with their students about prayer requests and pray together or assign the workshop leaders to lead the closing activity and prayer. If there is a large-group Closing, where all the students join together in music and prayer, use the suggestions found in options 1–3 for the format. Make sure that the workshop leaders know what time they need to be done by so everyone can gather quickly.

General

With any setting, Growing in Christ offers a variety of storytelling options. The supplemental Bible story posters are another tool to consider using in your rotation model. The story is written on the back of the poster for the leader to read out loud. Consider purchasing two sets of posters, cutting one up to create puzzles of each story for students to put together for review. Laminate the posters and puzzle pieces and they'll last longer.

Resources in the Teacher Tools packets can be separated and used in individual stations. The Bible Words Puzzle Books may be incorporated into a memory station for different ages, not just the group noted for. Other memory games included in the curriculum may be adapted for many age groups.

The Growing in Christ curriculum is flexible and can be adapted to meet your needs. It contains many resources that will allow you to create an exciting learning environment for children of all ages. It is not necessary to use everything every month, but you won't run out of options either.

Part 6: Overall Administration

Administrating a site-rotation Sunday School varies from the traditional model in a variety of ways. While the overall recordkeeping and promoting of the educational ministries for children is the same, working with volunteers and individuals is not. Recruitment for a site-rotation Sunday School program can be easier, but it still has its challenges. After all, site rotation's flexibility, shorter time commitments, and use of specialized roles make it more attractive to volunteers than the usual one-year commitment. However, because in most models individuals do not commit to an entire year of teaching, recruitment and training continues year round.

Communication is critical when working with a larger group of volunteers. Always let them know what is expected of volunteers, maintain contact lists, and stay in touch. Files for each small group should be made available to your Shepherds when they come each week to pick up the supplies they will need. Individual stations or workshops will have their individual needs, but if there are supplies that need to be moved around, such as student handouts, Shepherds should receive these at the beginning of the education hour.

Reviewing curriculum pieces and separating out specific tools for the different stations is another role of a site-rotation administrator. Create a team or select a trusted volunteer staff person to do this sorting. Create a separate file for each story and station to allow for additional resources to be added regularly. Student packs are an excellent resource for the different workshops. Review what aspects from the student packs can be used in different settings. If there are resources that are not going to be used, send them home with your students for reinforcement in the home. Or use them as a basis for a home mailing to keep parents up to date on what is happening in the education hour and to recommend ways to reinforce each Sunday's lesson.